# THE
# VICTIM
# PANDEMIC

Overcoming Life's Tragedies

POLLY HARDER

Published by:
R.H. Publishing
3411 Preston Rd. Ste. C-13-146
Frisco, Texas 75034

Copyright © 2020, Polly Harder

ISBN#978-1-945693-46-5   paperback
ISBN#978-1-945693-50-2   eBook

All rights reserved under International Copyright Law. Written permission must be secured from the publisher to reproduce, copy, or transmit any part of this book.

Scriptures marked NAS are taken from the NEW AMERICAN STANDARD (NAS): Scripture taken from the NEW AMERICAN STANDARD BIBLE®, copyright© 1960, 1962, 1963, 1968, 1971, 1972, 1973, 1975, 1977, 1995 by The Lockman Foundation. Used by permission.

Scriptures marked KJV are taken from the KING JAMES VERSION (KJV): KING JAMES VERSION, public domain.

Scriptures marked NIV are taken from the NEW INTERNATIONAL VERSION (NIV): Scripture taken from THE HOLY BIBLE, NEW INTERNATIONAL VERSION ®. Copyright© 1973, 1978, 1984, 2011 by Biblica, Inc.™. Used by permission of Zondervan

Scriptures marked NKJV are taken from the NEW KING JAMES VERSION (NKJV): Scripture taken from the NEW KING JAMES VERSION®. Copyright© 1982 by Thomas Nelson, Inc. Used by permission. All rights reserved.

Scriptures marked NLT are taken from the HOLY BIBLE, NEW LIVING TRANSLATION (NLT): Scriptures taken from the HOLY BIBLE, NEW LIVING TRANSLATION, Copyright© 1996, 2004, 2007 by Tyndale House Foundation. Used by permission of Tyndale House Publishers, Inc., Carol Stream, Illinois 60188. All rights reserved. Used by permission.

Scriptures marked AMP are taken from the AMPLIFIED BIBLE (AMP): Scripture taken from the AMPLIFIED® BIBLE, Copyright © 1954, 1958, 1962, 1964, 1965, 1987 by the Lockman Foundation Used by Permission. (www.Lockman.org)

Scriptures marked ESV® are taken from The Holy Bible, English Standard Version®), copyright © 2001 by Crossway Bibles, a publishing ministry of Good News Publishers. Used by permission. All rights reserved.

# ACKNOWLEDGMENTS

Over the past 25+ years I have had the privilege of helping many individuals receive and maintain their freedom from some pretty devastating events they have experienced in their lives. At the time, I know they rejoiced, not only because of the victories that were finally gained, but also in the new freedom they walked in.

However, the Word of God says in Proverbs 11:25,
> "...whoever refreshes others will be refreshed."

The truth is, I have been able to rejoice with all of you, as well. When I see how the Lord has turned your mourning into morning—hope and joy rising up from the ashes—creating in you the glorious life He ordained for you to live from the very beginning—it not only changed you, but it has allowed me to see God's love and provision for every one of you. His continual faithfulness to each of you built my own faith more than you could ever know.

It is for this reason that I want to dedicate this book to all those who have trusted me with their stories. I pray you still walk in the victory God has given you to move forward in the glorious light of His precious Son, Jesus Christ.

Regardless of our circumstances, our positions, our finances, our losses and gains, we ARE and ALWAYS will be VICTORS—not victims—through Jesus Christ, our Lord and Savior!

Romans 8:35, 37 declares:

> "Who shall separate us from the love of Christ? Shall trouble or hardship or persecution or famine or nakedness or danger or sword? ... No, in all these things we are more than conquerors through him who loved us" (NIV).

The New Living Translation states it like this:

> "Can anything ever separate us from Christ's love? Does it mean he no longer loves us if we have trouble or calamity, or are persecuted, or hungry, or destitute, or in danger, or threatened with death? ... No, despite all these things, ***overwhelming victory*** is ours through Christ, who loved us."

> "But thanks be to God!
> He gives us the victory
> through our
> Lord Jesus Christ"
> (1 Corinthians 15:57, NIV).

# TABLE OF CONTENTS

INTRODUCTION..................................................................9

Chapter 1
AM I A VICTIM?................................................................17

Chapter 2
NATURAL REACTIONS TO LIFE'S TRAGEDIES.........................25

Chapter 3
WHY DO I KEEP REPEATING THE SAME THING?.....................37

Chapter 4
ARE FEELINGS TRUSTWORTHY.........................................47

Chapter 5
"AS A MAN THINKS IN HIS HEART, SO IS HE."........................51

Chapter 6
NEGATIVE EMOTIONS PRODUCE PHYSICAL
ILLNESSES.....................................................................61

Chapter 7
OVERCOMING PAST PATTERNS.........................................71

Chapter 8
FINDING COMPLETE FREEDOM.........................................79

CONCLUSION..................................................................................85

SPEAK—BELIEVE—RECEIVE.........................................................89

BIBLIOGRAPHY............................................................................135

# INTRODUCTION

Bob and Eleonora went to their granddaughter's recital. It was so rewarding to see their precious one on the stage performing. It wasn't until a few days later, when Bob got a sore throat and began to cough that the trouble started. He grew worse, so they took him to the doctor, who immediately had him rushed to the hospital. After several weeks of torture, Bob died with the Coronavirus Disease (Covid 19). As horrific and unexpected as his death was, she couldn't honor him with a funeral. But the even bigger reality now was Eleanor had to deal with the overcoming fear that she and the other members of her household would also get this deadly disease and die.

---

Sharon had been a Registered Nurse for 20+ years. She loved her job. Actually it really wasn't even a job to her. She wanted to serve those who were ill, and she took great joy in being able to comfort them in any way she could while they were sick. She worked at one of the major hospitals in her city. However, all that changed when the intake of patients went to beyond capacity and the intensive care unit was also filled. The staff's shifts became endless, as they all worked around the clock to help those who were infected with the deadly Coronavirus. Even when masks were implemented, many of the staff knew it was too late for them. Sharon not only died, but so did four of her fellow co-workers.

---

Susan and Joe were both at work in the business they owned. Suddenly the sky turned black. Susan immediately turned on the weather channel only to discover that an F5 tornado was just two miles south of their kid's school. Susan grabbed Joes' arm as the alarms began to sound. She frantically yelled, "We've got to get the kids," but Joe stopped her and said, "There's no time. Now, we need to get to shelter." Within 15 minutes the wind had stopped. It was all over. Well, the tornado was over, but the life changes Joe and Susan would soon encounter were just beginning. For what they were about to learn was that the school had been demolished. None of the students or teachers had survived. Needless to say, they and the entire community were devastated.

---

Jane came from a broken and abusive home. When her dad was home, he was either asleep—drunk—or yelling at her or her mother. Because of his physically abusive ways, she ran away from home at 16, and by 17, was living with her boyfriend. Several months later, when his drinking raged out of control and he was now becoming physically abusive to her, she cried out, "Why me? What did I do to deserve this again?"

---

Billy was a good and responsible student. He was 11 years old, two years older than his brother, Steve, when his mom decided to go to nursing school in the evenings. Her full-time job during the day was not enough to support them, but she knew nursing could be a way to provide for them once she got the training and was certified. The neighbor, who lived a few doors down, went to the same church she and her family went to. This neighbor had a daughter who did babysitting. So Billy's mom felt it would be safe to hire her to watch her boys. Little did she know that the daughter battled with drugs and immoral sexual desires, which she inflicted upon both Billy and Steve.

At first, Billy thought it was cool that a senior in high school would be interested in him. After all, she did tell him that she "loved him and wanted him." But if this were the case—the truth—then why did he feel so badly? Why did he start to be so overcome with shame and guilt? Why did he want to hide when she came over?

Billy thought he would be able to get over this as he grew older, but 20 years later, he still carried this guilt and shame and struggled with being able to trust and have healthy relationships with the opposite sex. In fact, to protect himself, he began to dabble in another sexual lifestyle.

---

Amy and John decided to take a long-needed vacation. Money was short so they went to a city in a neighboring state, Las Vegas, Nevada. After shopping and having a wonderful day seeing the sites along the strip, they chose to walk back to their hotel. Suddenly, they saw people dropping like flies and the horrific sound of a machine gun firing shot after shot. They also dropped to the ground. After the shots ended, she looked over at John. Unfortunately, he had been shot in the leg and was lying in a pool of his own blood. In total shock and unbelief, she cried out for help from those who were around them. The police were only minutes away and ambulances had been dispatched to come and get the wounded to the local hospital.

---

Allan was suddenly called to the hospital because his mother had been rushed there. When he arrived his wife told him she had been just fine, but suddenly grabbed her chest. She knew she was having another heart attack, so she immediately called 911. They didn't have a long wait at the hospital before the doctor came to them with the news … his mother was gone. Allan thought, "Are you ever prepared for these things? Even when this was her third heart attack?" Coping as best as he could to make the funeral arrangements, he was shocked when the death certificate arrived and it stated the cause of death was the Coronavirus. He called the hospital to clear this up, but was told, "We are being 'paid' to state every cause of death at this time as the Coronavirus." Allen tried to reason with her, but to no avail. Now he not only had to deal with the death of his mom, but the reason for her death was an outright lie!

---

Unfortunately, especially in today's pandemic crisis events, these kinds of scenarios are not uncommon. At any turn, one can experience something that not only has the potential of changing their own life forever, but their family's lives, as well. This Corona pandemic, the anger and violent riots and protest outbreaks, along with the widespread natural disasters the world is experiencing from tornados, fires, hurricanes, floods, pestilence and the like, with years of cleanup and devastation many today are faced with, know what it truly means to be a victim.

In fact, because of this deadly virus, the racial violence, all of these natural disasters, all of the sexual crimes, sex-trafficking and abuses, along with the mass shootings that are happening on a daily or regular basis, it has caused the victim crisis to now escalate to that of major proportions—actually a pandemic level. We've passed the epidemic level when the entire world was shut down, as we all were asked to stay indoors on a "lockdown" for extended periods of time.

In these kinds of situations and other abusive relationships, everyone involved, whether it's accidental or on purpose—whether innocent or guilty—become a victim. All victims, sooner or later, will end up making decisions (as a man thinks) that will have the power to keep them in the same role—the same position—a victim.

Even before this global attack, whether young or old, we've all, had an opportunity to go through unfortunate circumstances. Many of our family members experienced world-effecting events as they battled in World War I and II, Japan, Vietnam, Afghanistan, Iran/Iraq, Israel, and even the

Great Depression that hit the U.S. However, the harder and more difficult the circumstances are doesn't always determine the emotional response from the individual. There is no question that when the outcome that one faces includes death, the seriousness of the matter goes to an entirely different level.

For example, I've counseled those whose injuries have been as far apart as having been sexually assaulted as a young child, to those who, because of a car accident, broke their leg and couldn't deal with the pain afterwards when they tried to exercise. Ordinarily, you wouldn't put these two in the same category. However, how each one handles their pain—emotional or physical—depends on several things, even if the main root of the injury remains the same.

The depth of the injury or offense will be determined by whether or not they can manage their thoughts. The Word is clear, "As a man thinks in his heart, so is he" (Proverbs 23:7, NIV). This verse lets us know that our thought process is very important, not only in the big things, but in our everyday events. There is no doubt what happened to you could be classified as offensive, but only you can decide—choose—whether or not you will actually be offended.

Now you may be thinking, "How does one get over or change their thinking when the world is under attack, people are dying, when there is such chaos in the government because the democrats and republicans are battling it out, and the news media has taken sides in such a manner that you don't even know whether or not what you are hearing from them is the truth?"

These are very valid questions? When there is chaos all around you, regardless of the source, how do you manage your thinking? Why is our thinking process the root of whether or not we stay a victim?

Offense—injury—is definitely a key weapon the enemy uses. And FEAR is usually right there with every attack. Why is fear so powerful? It's because fear has the ability to paralyze us. When we are wounded emotionally or injured, it's hard to think ... then react ... clearly and productively. If the offense or injury isn't dealt with quickly, this unproductive thinking has the potential of becoming a lifestyle. Thus, we have not only 'been' a victim, we now have 'become' a victim.

When we become a victim, it doesn't take long to think, then act, like one. This kind of thinking is referred to as a victim mentality. The damaging effects of this mentality can even motivate one to take drastic measures to end the emotional pain. These kinds of thoughts only have one direction—a downward spiral into a state of serious depression. This depression can lead one to believe all is hopeless, which leads to an even more dangerous way of thinking—to end it all through suicide.

Because of the "staying in" government lockdown, along with the overwhelming sense of panic and fear, the feelings of hopelessness and depression have escalated and the suicide rate is at an all-time high. Both drug and alcohol usage is off the charts.

- Why is it that we can't manage or control these kinds of devastating thoughts?
- Especially if it comes to wanting to bring an end to our lives?
- Why is it that when one 'grows up' or should at least 'out-grow' these traumatic events, they can't just "Get Over It?"

This is what many ministers, as well as psychological doctors, advise their counselees or patients to do today ... "Just Get Over It" or "Move On!" However, if you've ever had an addiction—smoking, over-eating, drugs, pornography, and so on—were you able to just "Get over it?" We know the answer to that question most of the time and for most of us, is "NO!"

In order to change our thinking, ideas, and desires there is a necessary process—whether it's in a specialized small group, counseling, therapy, or whatever—there is a process that one must go through. It's a rebuilding ... a rethinking of the events that have taken you down the path you're already on or about to go down. It's exchanging those thoughts with the truth of God's Word. His Word is full of promises that not only let us know the plan He has for us, but that He is all the while to work and to will His good pleasure in our lives. (Jeremiah 29:11, Philippians 2:13).

Regardless of the circumstances we have encountered, yes, as painful and devastating as life can get, we can live victoriously. God's ways are higher than ours, and when we let go of our thoughts and receive His thoughts, which are also higher than ours, we will live the life He designed especially for us. (Isaiah 55:8-9). A life that is full of hope, a future and a prosperous destiny in Him.

The "Good News" is you can become whole again. You can be stable in your emotions and healthy in all your decisions, regardless of when the event or trauma occurred. Time, in this case, cannot hold you back or prevent you from healing.

How is this possible? It's because this plan (God's plan) of recovery will help you define the reasons you think and react the way you do. It will help you if you've become a victim to get off of this vicious cycle and turn you into someone who is victorious instead.

Nothing is impossible with God. And His plan from the very beginning was to give you a hope, not harm you, to prosper you, and give you a future. (Jeremiah 29:11).

The Word says in 3 John 1:2,
> "Beloved, I wish above all things that thou mayest prosper and be in health, even as thy soul prospereth." (KJV).

One of the key words in this verse is "even." In other words, we are not going to be healthy or prosperous in other areas of our lives if our soul is not well. Your soul is your mind, will and emotions. This verse makes it clear that when our thoughts, which lead to our emotions, are not well ... the outcome is not one of peace, health and happiness.

Are you ready to receive a prosperous soul? One that leads to an overcoming, victorious life—even through life's pain, trials and pitfalls?

Then let's begin.

CHAPTER 1

# AM I A VICTIM?

This question would be easy to answer today because of what we have all experienced through this virus that has attacked the world as we once knew it. However, if you have lived for very many years, you would probably agree that you have had other opportunities to be a victim, as well.

Merriam Webster's Dictionary defines a victim as,

- "one that is acted on and usually adversely affected by a force or agent (the schools are *victims* of the social system);
- one that is injured, destroyed, or sacrificed under any of various conditions (a *victim* of cancer, a *victim* of the auto crash, a murder *victim*);
- one that is subjected to oppression, hardship, or mistreatment (a frequent *victim* of political attacks);
- one that is tricked or duped (a con man's *victim*);
- a living being sacrificed to a deity or in the performance of a religious rite."[1]

Other sources refer to a victim as someone who has been harmed, lost, or destroyed. Someone who is the object of abuse, criticism, or ridicule.

# DEFINING THE ROLE OF A VICTIM

Until this current virus attack, maybe you've never really felt like a victim, but the truth is we've all been in situations or events with other individuals that were less than positive. Whether you were the outcast in your brothers and sisters relationships, you battled with bullies at school, were misunderstood and rejected by friends, a boyfriend or your mate, or you've have had to work with obstinate and contrary individuals on your job, we all have personally known or watched others being treated differently, even unfairly, for some reason or another.

Peer pressure to "fit in" isn't just something you experience in your home as a youngster or in the lower level school system. At college level there is another form of "fitting in" that involves being accepted into a sorority or a fraternity. There are many organized groups for every event—sports, music, drama, cheerleading, and so on. "Fitting in" or "being good enough" is something we learn about at a very young age, and how we see ourselves comes as a result of whether or not we qualify. Are we valuable? Do we have any self-worth? If we don't believe we do—we've already experienced what it feels like to be a victim.

Now you may be thinking that's just competition, which is good for one to succeed. Healthy competition does keep us moving forward at times when we may want to quit. However, too many times it still involves choosing who belongs and who doesn't.

Just the other day, I had someone answer a question I asked them with, "Well, I wasn't one of the ones ever chosen to be on someone's team." Unfortunately, this answer didn't have anything to do with what I had asked them or what we were talking about. I thought to myself, "This explains some of the actions/reactions I see coming from this individual at times."

The sad part is, they have been out of this kind of environment for over 50 years. Yet, here is a perfect example of how devastating those emotions of rejection and not feeling wanted or accepted can still be, regardless of how long ago it happened or one's age.

These are the areas and events from our pasts that keep us in the role of a victim. It keeps us in a certain method of thinking that every event that happens from then on gets cycled through. It's like a flour sifter, only instead of refining the flour and making it better, this sifter has become dirty, partially blocked, maybe even polluted.

Is it any wonder that you cannot have a positive conversation with some individuals if or when constructive comments are needed or involved? Or if there is a conflict in ideas? Immediately their sifter tells them this is criticism. Usually at this point, there isn't a productive or healthy conversation that follows.

One of the things I've discovered since I've been counselling this younger generation or millennials is they don't want to or know how to deal with any kind of direct, personal questions, let alone conflict. So they shut down, run away, or ignore any and all of the individuals involved—regardless of how long or how well they knew them before the conflict. Even if the friendship had been a good one, for years, they just don't respond anymore to texts, calls, or any other form of communication. Shutting them out of their lives forever somehow seems to be the answer for them.

Is it wrong for people to deal with issues differently? Is there only one way to overcome negative, contradicting feelings? The answer to both of these is "No." We are all created uniquely. However, the bottom line is, these thoughts and feelings have to be dealt with. Shutting an individual out, or shoving something down on the inside of us with the inner thought, "I don't care" or "This doesn't matter," isn't the answer either. This is when it becomes absolutely necessary to look inward, examine our thoughts and motives and learn how to be able to find solutions that are not only healthy and productive to you especially, but also so that others aren't injured in your response as well.

# WHY ME?

As a counselor, I have been asked many times, "Why me?" Why did this situation have to happen to me?" Without going into the details or specifics of the incident(s), many times the outcome is just that—they are a victim. It's not just being in the wrong place at the wrong time. If this were true, how does a young child who is being molested by an older adult, whether it's a relative or not, be in the wrong place at the wrong time, especially when they are just trying to sleep in their own beds at night.

There are those who prey on others. However, if further investigations were done when it comes to incest or molestation, you would discover in most cases that the individual who is doing the molesting was also molested or victimized at some point in their lives.

Child abuse, sex trafficking and sexual violence statistics today are beyond what anyone could think or imagine, and being committed by individuals you would never suspect. In 2017, Alanna Vagianos posted and article on *HUFFPOST*. In it she claimed that, "Every 98 seconds, someone in the U.S. is sexually assaulted. That means *every single day* more than 570 people experience sexual violence in this country.[2]

*The National Sexual Violence Resource Center—Info & Stats For Journalists—STATISTICS ABOUT SEXUAL VIOLENCE* reports that, "One in four girls and one in six boys will be sexually abused before they turn 18 years old [(f)]; 34% of people who sexually abuse a child are family members; 12.3% of women … and 27.8% of men were age 10 or younger at the time of their first rape/victimization … 96% of people who sexually abuse children are male, and 76.8% of people who sexually abuse children are adults." [(n) 3fn]

When you understand that we have an enemy, the devil, who came to steal, kill and destroy, (John 10:10), I guess these statistics shouldn't be a surprise. Although it is a horrendous picture of how far our culture has moved away from the Word of God, and it also reflects the lack of Godly discipline and love we all are to walk and live in, statistics don't lie.

When you remove the 'd' from devil you get the root of every form of violence … evil. The difference of whether or not we allow these horrible incidents to label us or tell us "who" we are is now up to us. Will we let this circumstance define our worth or will we believe what God says about us and determine our worth because of "who" we are in Him?

Another horrendous tragedy that is overwhelming us today is the outrageous, unfair, unjust action that occurred against a black man in Minnesota. Any action of violence is hard to work through, but when it's enforced by the very ones who take an oath to protect us, no one can understand it. But more acts of violence will never be the answer. Two wrongs will never make a right. Now, as a result, even more have become victims as buildings, properties, and individuals are being injured and destroyed on a daily basis.

The amount of widespread devastation the world has encountered in the last few years, not only through this unprecedented virus, but the natural disasters like hurricanes, tsunamis, tornadoes, volcanos, wild fires, blizzards and the like are devastating. Hurricane Katrina hit New Orleans in 2005. In 2015, ten years later, photos were taken to show not only the reconstruction, but what was still needing much work. Dead trees were still standing in the marsh wetlands in south New Orleans, as well as a wrecked boat, shipping containers and debris. Today, if you looked at some of these photos and didn't know it was New Orleans, you would never guess that they were taken in the U.S.

I live in Dallas, Texas, and I remember well the events that followed Hurricane Harvey when it hit Houston in 2017. "Harvey caused at least 107 confirmed deaths: 1 in Guyana, and 106 in the United States. Total damage from the hurricane was estimated to be at $125 billion (2017 USD), making it among the costliest natural disasters ever in the

United States, comparable with Hurricane Katrina in 2005."[4] But there have been others ... on the east coast, as well as in Florida.

Then we look at the wild fires in California and the west coast. The U.S. is battling the effects of all of these disasters. *The New York Times* wrote on November 12, 2018, "The inferno that ravaged the wooded town of Paradise in northern California became the deadliest wildfire in the state's modern history on Monday when officials said they had discovered the remains of 13 more people, bringing the death toll to 42. The Butte County sheriff, Kory L. Honea, has said more than 200 people remain missing in and around the town, which sits in the foothills of the Sierra Nevada and was popular with retirees. The fire, which continues to rage in the hills and ravines east of the city of Chico, is also the most destructive fire in California history, with more than 7,100 structures destroyed, most of them homes. Fires whipped by strong winds were raging through thousands of acres of forests and chaparral in both Northern and Southern California on Monday, having already wiped out a town in the Sierra Nevada and forced the evacuation of tens of thousands of residents west of Los Angeles."[5]

Many of my friends who live in those areas had to move to safer places during these fires as they continued to ravage the areas. Thankfully, their homes were not destroyed, but they testified you could smell the smoke for many, many months, and it was painful and difficult to look at the massive destruction of those homes and land around them that had been completely destroyed.

What about the below zero weather in the northern states this past winter, with hundreds of inches of snow. Temperatures were so severe they told pet owners to not let their animals go outside for any reason. It would be like stepping on dry ice, which would burn their paws.

Nature is one of the biggest weapons in creating victims when these disasters hit. All of these mentioned are just a small example of the U.S. disasters. The world has experienced many more that are just as devastating—some may even be worse. Then, where do you even begin to talk about the mass shootings that seem to be happening more and more. We all remember the devastation that hit America on April 20, 1999, when those two teenagers gunned down their classmates and teachers at Columbine High School in Littleton, Colorado. They killed 15 people and wounded 24. This violence sent shock waves through our nation—as we tried to comprehend the cause of ones' thinking to do such a thing, especially at a school.

While we often consider Columbine to be the first school shooting, there has been a shockingly large number of school shootings before that tragic event. In fact, the very first school shooting was in the 18th century.

These acts of outrage weren't just limited to the schools, as we have witnessed by what has happened in other cities across the U.S. These outrageous acts of violence have plagued our country since the early 20s. Those who were convicted of the murders gave excuses that range from just hatred of others, the day of the week, job/union strikes, mental illnesses and hatred of themselves.

If what some believe is the truth—mental illness is the cause—then we can see that in every case of these extreme acts of violence, they all were "off" in their thinking. No one in their "right" mind plots to do such evil. So we're back to the level of unproductive thinking the perpetrator must have had to be able to do such an evil act against people they never even knew.

The victims in all of these cases are more than those who were killed or injured. Their families and friends, the communities they happened in, and even the families of the sick individuals who were at fault all have the opportunity to fall into the category of being a victim.

So the biggest question now is, if I've been a victim …
How do I move forward?
How do I process what happened in a healthy way?
Is it possible to think on these things and still be able to think in a healthy way, too?

CHAPTER 2

# NATURAL REACTIONS TO LIFE'S TRAGEDIES

In situations like the ones mentioned in chapter one, when we are affected personally, the truth is we are victims. Abuse, criticism, and harm, whether it's physical or mental, is something that has to be dealt with. Different people respond differently to their circumstances.

Some decide the best way to handle certain negative situations is to shove things down on the inside of them or by thinking they can ignore them. However, this is not a healthy way to overcome these areas of pain. At the time it may feel like we are gaining the victory, and if years have passed without having to recollect the incidents, one may "feel" like they are over it or they have overcome the incident. However, all it takes is another similar incident, and those same emotions get stirred up again, all the while showing us that we have not overcome anything. Burying something doesn't make it go away—just because it is out of sight.

Another similar way to shoving it down on the inside of us or hiding it is to "pretend" it never happened in the first place. A process of denying it ever happened goes into effect. When abusive traumas happen to children, it's easier for them to pretend that it never happened. Why would this method seem to work for them for a season?

Well, for a child, it's okay to pretend. Girls play with their dolls and men play with soldiers, etc. They know what it is to make-up things as they play. So sometimes, by pretending these things didn't happen, it seems "logical" to a child's way of thinking. However, when one becomes an adult, pretending is no longer a healthy option. Sooner or later, one will have to remove and release the hidden emotions that have attached themselves to the unfortunate events in their earlier years.

Others don't try to shove it down, but actually live it out every day in every circumstance. These are the individuals you have to "walk on egg shells" with to be around. They are overly sensitive and cannot under any circumstances receive proper correction or direction. Everything is criticism to them, and they respond accordingly. Usually, most conversations, especially if they have a serious nature, end up in some form of argument—voices raised, cursing, even stomping out of the room for effect. Anger is their friend. It allows them permission to withdraw from any given situation, rather than facing it. To them, there is no such thing as conflict resolution.

Many will choose to ignore it, but live isolated and depressed. They could be very happy living in a one bedroom unit, because usually, they never want to get out of bed. Depression or having feelings of despair can be very dangerous if not treated. Unfortunately, drugs seem to be what the "Doctors order," but it's obvious if the drugs helped, the warning on any and all drugs that are used for depression wouldn't read, *"May cause serious depression and lead to suicide. If/when this occurs, consult your doctor immediately."*

How could a drug that is supposed to help with depression and/or thoughts of suicide make you more suicidal? What is the benefit of that? Plus, there are always many other side-effects that can occur, but again, the doctors tell you, "No problem," because they will just give you a prescription for another drug.

Another disaster the world is facing in an even greater measure today is suicide. Because of the lockdown the world has been under due to the spread of the virus, depression is at an all-time high. And not only just being depressed, but taking it further by committing suicide. Its death statistics far outweigh the deaths from the virus that has attacked us.

According to the National Institute of Mental Health, "Suicide is a major public health concern. Suicide is among the leading causes of death in the United States. As stated in an earlier chapter, based on recent nationwide surveys, suicide in some populations is on the rise."[6] This article went on to give the statistics for the different age groups who had committed the most suicides. Ages 25-34 were the third largest, with ages from 55-64 being the second highest, and the ages from 45-54 were the largest group.

One's mental health is based solely on how one thinks. These statistics tell us how easily someone can believe the wrong ideas, and thus, create the wrong thoughts, even to the point of believing death is the answer for them. The biggest problem here is when you continue to make poor choices, why wouldn't you continue to go around the same mountain or path. It's this same pattern that convinces one to believe that nothing will ever change, so why should they continue to live. To them ... moving on isn't even an option.

Anytime one battles with thoughts that lead to negative, unproductive emotions, more than likely they will make poor decisions in every other area of their lives, as well. Why? Because even when they know the outcome won't be good, they know how to live like a victim. Most turn to something, drugs or alcohol, to try to camouflage their thoughts. Again the lie is that this will help, even if it's just for a while. However, the consequences of becoming an addict only add to the problem. Drugs or alcohol will never be the answer—a permanent solution—to any emotional disorder.

"According to the National Survey on Drug Use and Health (NSDUH), 19.7 million American adults (aged 12 and older) battled a substance use disorder in 2017. That same year, 1 out of every 8 adults struggled with both alcohol and drug use disorders simultaneously."[7]

Our culture today wouldn't have to deal with the ever-increasing drug problem, including our opioid epidemic, if people were able to manage their thought life and emotional pain and consequences.

## UNDERSTANDING MY FEELINGS—REACTIONS

Can you relate to any of the ways to deal with painful circumstances that are mentioned above? Have you done the same to help you try to overcome a past injury or wound? At some time or another, we've all participated in some form of these kinds of scenarios. If not personally, then with someone we know—a family member, friend or co-worker.

In my many years of counseling, I've heard all of the above reasons for one acting like they do, so these types of feelings and then reactions aren't new. The enemy may try to tell you that you're the only one who feels this way, or no one else in your family deals with this, or no one will understand what you're going through, but the truth is, we've all had the opportunity to shut others out and close ourselves off from the world.

Why? Why does isolation or just shutting down emotionally seem to be the answer? It's because fear is now involved. We're afraid of any kind of relationship. The lie we believe is, if we remove ourselves from others, we won't get hurt. This may be partially true, especially if you don't know how to choose healthy people to be your friends or support group, but the pain of loneliness or not belonging will set in soon after. Again, this scenario has the opportunity to convince you that you have to live life alone, you're not loved, valuable or worth anything, all of which can cause self-destructive thoughts that lead to unproductive actions.

So then it's our decision—which pain is easier to tolerate—but remember, neither removes it. And now, maybe even worse, the door you've opened to fear is lying to you about your real future.

# HEREDITARY FACTORS

Many times, hereditary plays a big role in being a victim. If your parents battle with a victim mentality, and they were the ones who trained you in the way you should go, chances are you think like they do … thus, you also think like a victim.

We see this played out especially because of the environment one lives in. If you're in a wealthy neighborhood, the likelihood of a drive-by shooting is much slimmer than if you lived in an economically depressed neighborhood. Today, gangs can come from every form of habitat, it just seems that they "play" rougher and for keeps in the socially depressed ones. A gang in a well-to-do area may be just that of peer pressure groups—those who pick on or verbally abuse others because they don't fit into their group. These can also get violent, but usually physical involvement is in the form of fighting, rather than pulling a weapon on someone.

I recently had a parent contact me about a situation his daughter was experiencing at school in another state. One of the toughest peer groups for kids in school today is with those who are struggling with their sexual identity. In her school there are quite a few lesbian girls who have formed their own group. Several of them are on the sports team that his daughter participates in as well. Due to the sensitivity of this subject I will say it like this: These girls had continually made aggressive sexual advances toward her and had sent her disturbing sexual texts.

This man's daughter, who is 12 years old, is a strong Christian, but she hadn't taken her authority over this situation out of fear. These girls had been very intimidating and had been quite successful with converting others to join their group after being distastefully and aggressively physical with them. When her dad saw the texts, he asked her why she hadn't said anything to him. She confessed she was afraid. He assured her she just needed to make it clear she was not like them, and they should mind their own business.

The next day he was called to come to the school. The problem: When his daughter tried to stand up for herself and her Christian beliefs, she was deemed the one causing the trouble. She was asked to leave the school for the day. I might add that the teacher involved in the matter, who dismissed her for the day, was also lesbian.

Many times victims of rape, sexual assault, family molestation, incest, and other forms of physical and emotional abuse or assault will choose the same sex as a safe measure. However, because of the guilt and shame associated with these actions, many don't ever tell anyone that they are happening in order for them to get help. Or in some cases, one of the parents is well aware of what the other parent is doing, but won't stand up for the child's benefit. In either situation, who does the child get help from when both parents are willing participants?

"Nationally-reported statistics regarding incest may be inaccurate because incest is often concealed by victims and not discussed at large in society. Survivors may be hesitant to come forward because of guilt, shame, fear, social and familial pressure, and/or coercion from the perpetrator. Research shows that 46% of children who had been raped had been assaulted by a family member or close relative."[8]

The article goes on to say that, "the younger victims of incest are most often assaulted by people in a trusted position, and therefore are led to believe the lies, explanations, and threats of this person. These perpetrators may lead the child into believing it is a learning experience that all children must go through. Some victims, especially depending on how young they were when molested, may not even know that what is being done to them is wrong."[9]

In the past few years I've had the opportunity to counsel women from several different non-American cultures. These women are taught they are to be protectors of their husbands, regardless of the emotionally and sometimes physical abuse they are dealing with. In the beginning of our sessions, they were very afraid of even discussing the immense grief and torment they were experiencing. Phrases like "that's just the way it is in our culture" or "men will be men" was supposed to be an answer for them.

Obviously, no one gets healed emotionally using that way of thinking. And if parents are to be the role models for their children, what is it exactly you're teaching them? Having healthy relationships and being able to understand your value and worth also isn't part of this kind of training.

However, regardless of one's nationality, the scars, guilt and shame are something they will eventually have to be freed from if they are going to function and think clearly about themselves and their actions toward others. More times than not, these dysfunctions are passed down from generation to generation. This brings us to another hereditary factor the Bible refers to as generational curses.

## GENERATIONAL CURSES

A generational curse isn't something that the American church talks much about today. And yes, I am well aware that according to Scripture Jesus became the curse for us because it's written in Galatians 3:13,

> "But Christ has rescued us from the curse pronounced by the law. When he was hung on the cross, he took upon himself the curse for our wrongdoing. For it is written in the Scriptures, 'Cursed is everyone who is hung on a tree.'" (NLT).

He became the curse that sin caused, separating us from God the Father. How one thinks, based on their upbringing, is another subject all together. Just recently I had the pleasure of working with a Nigerian Pastor on his book. In the book he explained the very beginning of slavery, not only in Africa, but in the West Indies. In fact, it was Willie Lynch from the West Indies, who had not only run a very successful farm with the aid of slaves, but who later came to America to teach the Virginia plantation owners how to "manage" their slaves.

According to this pastor's research, "Willie Lynch warned the Virginians that the evil, 6-point equation he had developed had to be mastered and transmitted as a perpetual legacy to citizens in every generation to keep their economic advantage. Long-range planning was paramount and successive generations had to understand this process ..."[10]

Even though this pastor goes into detail about Lynch's 6-points in his book, which are definitely evil, they are also too inhumane and unbearable for me to quote in this book. The extreme, emotional cruelty required to execute its mandate is beyond imagining.

Were slaves victims? Absolutely! And praise God for all those who stood up against it to bring national freedom to these individuals. Yet, because of the thinking methods that were instilled, many still act like victims, even though for them and several of their past generations they weren't under the same system or control. Why does one still want to keep themselves bound, when freedom has been established?

This makes me think of how an elephant is trained. Have you ever been to the circus or some place where you've seen a huge, grown elephant that can weigh anywhere between 5,000 to 14,000 pounds chained to a tiny metal ball? How or why doesn't this elephant run away? Obviously, that metal ball would be no challenge to this elephant. It's because when this elephant was young, the ball weighed much more than what this baby animal was able to move. Now, even though he far outweighs the ball, he still believes he can't move it—so why try? His mindset holds him bound by the same belief.

In the early days of slavery, chains held them bound. But after the chains were removed and freedom came, along with their liberation, why did the mindset not change? Especially when generations have passed without knowing this attack personally?

Another example of being in chains is to be yoked. God's plan for mankind was to never carry the burdens or for us to be yoked to anything destructive. He tells us is Matthew 11:28-30,

> "Come to me, all who labor and are heavy laden, and I will give you rest. Take my yoke upon you, and learn from me, for I am gentle and lowly in heart, and you will find rest for your souls. For my yoke is easy, and my burden is light." (ESV).

When we let God be in charge, trusting the Holy Spirit to lead us and guide us in all truth, we can rest, not only in our souls—mind, will and emotions—but physically, as well. We can be healed in our thinking process to forget the past. We are new creatures in Christ; the old has passed away. We were not created to just function in a life that is filled with dysfunction.

Unfortunately, slavery wasn't the only horrific bondage mankind has suffered. There was another man, who had many of these same beliefs. The same thinking patterns of one race being higher than another. His name was Adolf Hitler. Hitler rose in power to such an extent that he had many follow him in the brutal killings/execution of another innocent people group—the Jews. How does one justify and convince others that one race is superior to another? Well, unfortunately, Hitler succeeded at every point, and the death of six million Jews prove it!

In both of the above scenarios, it didn't matter whether you were man, women or child. What mattered was ones' race. But what about the discrimination and unequal thinking that existed and still exists today for women in many countries of the world? Many times, false religious rituals and demon gods were the culprits in creating these victims. Even today, who helps them with the emotional issues, traumas, devastating stories, sexual abuse, their children being sold for marriage and having sexual relations when they are 2-3 years old? Who helps them with the things they've witnessed that have happened to their own relatives, mothers, sisters, and wives? What has allowed these individuals to know their worth or value in order for their thought process to change and grow and be healthy?

In this pastor's book, he relates the black man's journey in slavery to the story of Moses. He writes,

> "The Hebrew housewives were the heroines of the day because the men had been reduced into hapless economic units in the Egyptian system. The application that was used in ancient Egypt was so effective that there was no human solution. The Hebrew mothers had been doing such a thorough job of raising docile slaves that the process had gone uninterrupted for 430 years ...
>
> "We must note that salvation could not come through anyone raised by the system. Moses was not brought up in a Hebrew home! He was not subject to the bite of the devil's calculations, and he did not have the emotional and cognitive limitations that came with it. The Hebrew slaves were another matter. Even when millions of them were liberated from Egypt, the Egyptian bondage buried deep inside each one of them could not be removed. The process of reconversion from the slavery mentality and sub-human nature back into a wholesome person was tough. Only two or three people were revitalized out of the three to five million freed slaves of the Exodus ...
>
> "Moses discovered that multiple problems emerged whenever slaves were liberated from the bondage environment. Liberated slaves often vote for a return to bondage after tasting the responsibilities that go with freedom. An animalized man is like a domestic pet or a field donkey whose purpose has been redefined to serve a master. The restoration of a slave would

require the waking of dead brain cells and the conditioned slave would naturally resist the exercise."[11]

In other words, God knew how important it was for Moses, if he was to deliver the Israelites, to not have any concept or thinking capacity of what it was like to be a slave. In this situation, there would be no generational history, background, traits, images, or curses to overcome, remove or want to return to, if or when difficult situations arose.

The Israelites are a perfect example of the difficulty it takes for one to change their thinking mode. It took almost four generations of being—living free—before they were ready to go in and possess the land God had promised them.

Today, we hear the questions asked, "When will things get back to normal?" The truth is, many didn't like the way their lives were before this happened, so why would they even want to go back? It goes back to our thinking patterns.

When Moses delivered the Israelites and God provided for them daily, the moment they got tired of their manna, they wanted to go back to Israel. They were slaves, beaten and mistreated, with unrealistic goals for them to achieve, but they were fed … so when food became unacceptable … their old way of thinking took over, and now they wanted to return to an unhealthy and dangerous life.

This is why God's Word is specific. When He says, "As mankind thinks in their heart, so are they!" it's the truth. After you've been trained for so long to think a certain way, even when it's wrong, and somewhere within you, **you know it's wrong**, you have to be willing to change your thoughts … submit your thoughts to line up with God's Word. This is the only way for one to change and grow healthily, which allows one to continue to move forward in victory.

I wonder if Dr. Martin Luther King, Jr. were still alive today what his reaction would be to the violent events that are occurring in cities all across America due to the death of George Floyd. Please understand me ... there was nothing right about the treatment and what happened to Mr. Floyd. And I pray for his family. But the death and destruction of so many others, does not change the injustice of his death. We have all heard the saying that "Two Wrongs Don't Make a Right!"

When Dr. King marched or held protests, they always emphasized "Peace." For any of us who were involved in the civil rights movement in the late 60s and early 70s, it is disturbing to see how far we have regressed in handling things, for both blacks and whites, and every other nationality involved.

Dr. King was one of the most powerful examples for every race to see how to handle unfair, victim-provoking actions against any individual. He continued to walk in love and forgiveness. He stated, "Darkness cannot drive out darkness; only light can do that. Hate cannot drive out hate; only love can do that. The time is always right to do what is right."

Dr. King truly was a hero, demonstrating the work of God on earth. It is no surprise that his messages still resound in the halls of history today. Let us not forget his example. When he said, "Free at last; Free at last, Thank God Almighty, We're free at last," was he talking about more than being free in the natural? Was he talking about knowing who you are in God, and truly thanking Him for delivering us from any of the bondages and unfair situations that life can bring?

The key to moving forward is to continue to look forward to the new thing God is going to do in the world today, and in our lives, regardless of what happens around us.

God didn't bring this upon the world. It is evil, and remember that is the "d"evils work.

However, God's Word is clear,

"As for you, you (devil) meant evil against me, but God meant it for good in order to bring about this present outcome, that many people would be kept alive [as they are this day]" (Genesis 50:20, AMP).

CHAPTER 3

# WHY DO I KEEP REPEATING THE SAME THING?

I know we have all heard the saying, "Monkey see—monkey do!" Wikipedia says that "Monkey see, monkey do is a pidgin-style saying that appeared in American culture in the early 1920s. The saying refers to the learning of a process without an understanding of why it works. Another definition implies the act of mimicry, usually with limited knowledge and or concern for the consequences."[12]

As this saying implies, many times we just do what we've seen our parents, siblings or those responsible for our upbringing do. If the role model was a good one, the results will most likely be positive, but when the role model wasn't a good one, the battle to overcome and to change must begin.

Today, we also have the massive effect of social media delivering its unimpressive, false, degrading influence on those who have so easily become addicted to it. The phone has become such a valuable piece of one's life that even in a restaurant, a family of four has no communication with one another because each individual is on their own device.

Many times, there is a lack of proper supervision for the young adult, so with all the social areas being made available for them to participate in, who only knows what goes through their thinking processes. Plus, at their age, they don't know how to truly take every thought captive. This is why the drugs, cutting oneself, and suicide rate is so high for young adults.

So, with all these outside and home influences, the young adult has to try to understand why they think the way they do … and then act the way they do. Anger, bullying, outbursts, cursing and other aggressive forms of behavior are just signs that something is really going on deep within the individual. This doesn't just apply to children or young adults. If these poor thoughts and mindsets aren't dealt with, we will continue to see the same kind of behavior in grown adults.

Or, sometimes, we can see the opposite behavioral attitude—inferior, silent, a loner, one who doesn't mix well with others, runs from discipline or conflict. These individuals can be very passive, seemingly sweet people. However, these types don't do well with conflict. In fact, they run from it. If you have had to work on a team with individuals like this, you know how frustrating it can be when their standard answer is, "Whatever you think." Or, "I don't care!" That is, if they will even make a comment. Usually, they can't handle unruly employees and definitely can't administer any kind of discipline or punishment. They don't make very good managers because they can hardly manage themselves.

So, when this occurs, you have to be the one to deal with it because they either can't or won't. Either scenario is a sure sign there is trouble in their thinking and thought-processing abilities, which has come from some form of their past, unproductive treatment.

As an example of this, years ago I was asked to be the manager of a Christian unwed mothers' home that needed some help. My supervisor and her supervisor had both had abortions and wanted to do something to help others, which was very commendable. However, the home was a dysfunctional mess, and it didn't take me long to discover why. There was no one in management who was willing to be in charge—a definite lack of supervision. So why wouldn't there be chaos when "no one" would step up and be in charge.

Within a short period of time, I had to discipline one of the women because she refused to accept the rules. She was rebellious, and

I don't know if she had accepted Christ or not, which was one of the key requirements for living there. After several warnings on my part, it came time to act upon her disrespectful ways to me and others in the home, along with her blatant disobedience in following the house rules.

By now this woman had delivered the baby. And one act of her rebellion was she refused to change the baby's diapers in the requested area. Instead, she would use the living room couch, which the baby peed on many times.

As soon as I called her into my office and tried to address the issues, she blew up at me with some lame excuse and immediately went to my boss. Unfortunately, my boss didn't support me. Eventually, at my request, she called a meeting with the three of us.

After a few minutes of the woman griping and complaining about her situation, which I remind you she was living there free of charge, my boss asked me if I had anything to say. I pulled out the instruction manual she had given me to follow when she hired me. I pointed to the section(s) where this woman was in violation. I asked my supervisor, "Is this our rule for the girls to follow or not?" She looked at me for a second and then started her answer with "Well …!" As far as I was concerned, the meeting didn't need to go any further than that.

The sad part is, my boss had been the one who had been in charge before they hired me. She could not manage, nor execute any kind of discipline, so the girls did whatever they wanted. This is why there was so much chaos. As it turned out, she had not only had several abortions, but she had also had a big problem with drugs, which led to being arrested several times. In other words, she had lived a pretty tough life. Her younger years were filled with horrible abuses, alcohol and drugs. Because of this, she couldn't discipline others without becoming abusive herself—so—she didn't discipline anyone.

This explained why the home was in such an unstable predicament when I first arrived. This also explained why this girl thought she could continue to get away with her abusive treatment to others and to not follow any of the rules. As a result, some of the others thought they didn't have to follow the rules either. It was definitely not a good situation.

Within a few months, I felt the Lord's leading to resign, which I did. A few weeks after I left, the home closed. What a shame. Obviously, she recognized she couldn't manage the home and needed help. That's why they hired me. However, to not support me or anyone else who would have been in management to bring peace and to put an end to the chaos, was just more evidence of her unhealed soul. This problem didn't just effect the unwed mother's home. She, her husband and her family also went to therapy every week for the same reason. She couldn't discipline her own children without becoming abusive either.

## CONTINUED MISTAKES

If our thinking doesn't change, why would the outcome change? In fact, I've heard that's the definition of insanity—doing things the same way, but expecting a different outcome. As long as we continue to think the same, we will continue to make the same mistakes, or "go around the same mountain." It becomes a viscous cycle that only causes one to get angrier or more abusive or to shut down even more.

So how do you change the way you think? Especially if you don't know why you think and feel the way you do? To change anything, many times you have to go back … you have to go back to the beginning. You have to identify what happened to cause your emotions to enslave you. Just as plants have roots that go deep into the soil, our thoughts also have roots. Sometimes when you look at pictures of the brain, it almost looks like trees or plants are growing in them.

Being able to identify the source is a key factor in knowing how to change one's thoughts to be free.

## THE ENEMY'S WEAPONS

It's also important to recognize that regardless of who the perpetrator was, you have another enemy. The Bible makes it clear in John 10:10 that the devil comes to destroy, but Jesus came to give us life.

> "The thief comes only to steal and kill and destroy; I came that they may have life, and have it abundantly" (John 10:10, NAS).

When you know that regardless of the action, which was meant for your harm, that God turns those things to our good, (Genesis 50:20), we have the strength and courage to face the unpleasant times in our lives in order to get the victory over our thinking.

Many times I've heard abused individuals confess, "I promised myself I would never do the things my dad did, or I won't say the same things my dad said to me to my kids … BUT I'm doing it!" So the same reason your dad did these things is now the same reason you are doing these things. He had probably been abused by his dad or a close relative, as well. And for the most part, when we do bad things, we are aware they are bad. This alone causes us to be angry, not only with the circumstances, but with ourselves, too. We don't like it, and as a result, we don't like us very much either.

One day while watching TBN, which is a Christian TV network, I heard Pastor Jentzen Franklin talking about this very thing. Pastor Franklin is the senior pastor of Free Chapel, a multi-campus church with a global reach. That day, on his television program Kingdom Connection, he summed up the works of the enemy and his attacks in one statement. "The enemy (satan) will prepackage an old weapon to use it on a new generation."[13] Think about that! Why does he have to continue to use the same thing as a weapon against you? It's because this is the only way he can work his old tricks; he cannot create anything new. If you continue to think the same things, using the same pattern, why would the outcome be any different?

There is only One Creator, God Himself. So the devil has to convince us another way. How does he do it? Usually he mixes a tiny bit of truth with his lie, so we will believe it. But the bottom line is—he lies. The Bible tells us satan is the father of lies. (John 8:44).

What kind of lies is the enemy telling you?

- "I'll never be able to get free of this addiction!"
- "My dad was right. I'll never amount to anything!"
- "I'm worthless!"
- "I'm a mess, a loser, beyond repair!"
- "Nobody loves me!"
- "I'm always going to have to do this alone!"
- "I can't trust anyone; I'm always hurt in the end."

There is a scene in the movie, *Pretty Woman*, with Richard Gere and Julia Roberts where she's telling him about her past. She had quit school and started working, but lost her job. All of which caused her to leave home, move around a lot and get into an unhealthy occupation to support herself. She said, "Once you hear something enough times, you begin to believe it's true." After hearing her story, he tells her he thinks she is beautiful and smart and she can accomplish whatever she desires. She then says, "Have you ever noticed, the bad stuff is easier to believe."

Why is the "bad stuff" easier to believe? It's because the enemy continually plays the same old messages in our heads. How many times a day do you hear the same thing … or you tell yourself the same thing? Before I learned to take every thought captive, when I would do something that was unusual for me, I would say, "How stupid was that, Polly?"

After a while, when we tell ourselves derogatory things, it's easy to begin to think that this is really who we are. Now, it's no longer just a stupid action, we do it because we actually believe we're the ones who are stupid.

The Bible tells us in 2 Corinthians 10:5,

"*Casting down imaginations*, and every high thing that exalteth itself against the knowledge of God, and *bringing into captivity every thought* to the obedience of Christ;" (KJV).

There is a reason we are to take control of our thoughts. They have power over our actions. What we see or are saying may be the facts, but the only truth is found in God's Word. Facts are temporary—subject to change—but God's Word is permanent—forever! When the same thoughts keep going through one's mind, over and over again, until they are now being spoken out of our mouths, you can see how powerful they can become. This is why the Word says,

"A good man out of the good treasure of his heart brings forth good; and an evil man out of the evil treasure of his heart brings forth evil. **For out of the abundance of the heart his mouth speaks**" (Luke 6:45, NKJV).

When we think something long enough, this is truly what we believe about ourselves. Soon these very thoughts are what we begin to speak. The power of "Life and Death" are in the tongue, (Proverbs 18:21), that's why Jesus cautioned us about our words and thoughts. These bad thoughts can be as addictive as drugs.

Addictions are one of the leading causes of abuse, both physical and verbal. Merriam Webster's Dictionary defines addiction as,

"The quality or state of being <u>addicted</u>, *addiction* to reading;

"<u>Compulsive</u> need for and use of a habit-forming substance (such as heroin, nicotine, or alcohol characterized by <u>tolerance</u> and by well defined physiological symptoms upon withdrawal; *broadly* : persistent compulsive use of a substance known by the user to be harmful without regard to consequences."

Other synonyms for addiction are: dependence, habit, and monkey.

If you were continually told you would never be able to do anything right or you were ugly or unwanted or a mistake, it doesn't take too many others—including your own "self-talk"—to convince you they're right.

I understand the power of self-talk because of my own and the recourse from it. When I grew up I had a couple of classmates who were jealous of me. I was raised in a rural area, but my mother worked in a larger city that was 15 miles east of the town we lived in. She managed an upscale boutique, and I was able to work along with her in the world of fashion. Going to markets and buying my wardrobe from the market samples were just some of the perks. It was quite the lifestyle for just a small-town girl, but unfortunately, these classmates were daily making derogatory remarks. Their comments were, "I just hate you; you always have something nice to wear," or "I hate you; you always look nice." Was I able to see they were jealous? Yes! Did it start to affect me that I was hated? ... Yes, it did.

Then the enemy lied to me, telling me that this wasn't the real reason they hated me. There was something wrong with me; that's why they hated me. So my way as a young adult to manage my thoughts was to tell myself, "I don't care what they think." Did this work? Well, I thought it was working until I realized I had become rebellious, and I was starting to make decisions that were not good ones. What had happened was, after

I had told myself for so long that I didn't care ... my subconscious came to believe it. Now, my decisions were reflecting just that, and the outcome from my self-talk caused the consequences of some of my decisions to be far from pleasant.

The truth is, the real power over you—good and bad—is still determined by YOU! It all comes down to being able to manage or take captive how you think and what you say about what you're thinking. You can either continue to "REHEARSE" your thoughts or the events and your situation OR you can "REPLACE" those thoughts with the truth, not allowing offense to be formed.

When you are emotionally healthy, understanding who you are in Christ, and Who They (the Godhead) are in you, you will discover it really doesn't matter what others say or do. It's just that now you are balanced in your thinking, not taking offense and forgiving others. Now, you don't have to continually tell yourself something that doesn't line up in God's Word about your true identity. You will no longer have a desire to go over the same thing, repeating it and telling everyone you know about "your" situation. Now you will stop the chatter and let your words be powerful in changing your life. In other words, there may come a season where we have to learn to just "Shut-Up!"

We are all different and uniquely created by a loving Father. Celebrate your differences ... learn to rejoice and be glad. Can you imagine what this world would be like if we all were the same? I wonder why "robots" just came to my mind?

CHAPTER 4

# ARE FEELINGS TRUSTWORTHY?

Most of the time, even when things seem to be going well, our feelings cannot be trusted. They are usually based on what's going on around us, which is always subject to change at a moment's notice. Not a very steady foundation.

As previously mentioned, the only sure foundation or truth this world has is the Word of God. The Bible says that Heaven and Earth will pass away, but God's Word will stand forever. (Isaiah 40:8; Matthew 24:35). This is why when we are trying to change anything about ourselves we know we can trust God's Word. We can lean on it. When we think on these things, both our outlook and our attitude are transformed. Our mind is renewed, which is what is supposed to happen when we read and study His Word. In fact, the Word tells us to think on these things:

> "Finally, brothers and sisters, whatever is true, whatever is noble, whatever is right, whatever is pure, whatever is lovely, whatever is admirable —if anything is excellent or praiseworthy—think about such things" (Philippians 4:8, NIV).

Now you might be thinking, "Well maybe others can think on "these things," but do you see what's happening in the world? Do you have any idea what I have to go through on a daily basis? I've lost my job, my business, my loved one because of this pandemic and these protesting outbreaks. This is not only unrealistic … it's impossible!"

When I hear these kinds of remarks, it's not that I don't understand their pain and what they're going through. But what I also understand is that their eyes are on what is going on around them and not on the truth. Most individuals, until they really have a chance to mature in the things of God, want to base their feelings on their circumstances, regardless of how big or small they are.

Good day—feeling happy!

Bad day—feeling depressed and down.

When we base our "feelings" on our outer circumstances or what's happening around us, we are actually giving them permission to take control—or be in charge.

The word "happy" originates from the Greek word "happenings." The Bible doesn't tell us to be happy. It tells us to be joyful. Joy is a decision. It's not based on what's happening around us or our circumstances. We choose—make a decision with our thoughts—to be joyful. The Word says,

"Do not be grieved, for the joy of the Lord is our strength" (Nehemiah 8:10, NAS).

So, in order to do this, we must know the truth of God's Word and then be willing to bring our soul—the mind, will and emotions—into agreement with it. We must discipline our thinking so we can see the good things God has promised us in His Word to come to fruition in our lives. And more times than not, FEAR has to be controlled in our thinking and emotions.

I've heard Kenneth Copeland, founder of KCM Ministries, which specializes in teaching the principles of Bible faith—prayer, healing, salvation and other biblical topics, give testimony many times about how he learned to fly. Without a plane, he would sit on a chair in his home and imagine the cockpit in front of him. He would picture the gauges and what they would need to read before he could even consider lifting the plane off the ground. He would imagine if the right engine went out, what would the gages tell him, and if he saw certain things, what action would he need to take? He meditated on exactly what the numbers on those gauges meant.

In telling this story, the one thing he stressed—implicitly—was you can never go by what you are feeling. Your feelings will kill you. You have to go by the truth in what the gauges are telling you. One degree difference can take you hundreds of miles in another direction—not just side to side, but if it's up or down, you could crash the aircraft.

This principle is true for us. When we meditate on God's Word, and know what it says, then when life's trials try to attack us, we have a gauge so to speak to look to for wisdom and an accurate direction as well. We have the power and ability to not be led by our feelings or emotions, even if it seems they are screaming loudly at us about the direction we should go. God's Word is on point. It will never lead us astray or let us down. Our feelings or emotions are not trustworthy or reliable, but His Word to us is and always will be.

Plus, He has given us the Holy Spirit, the Spirit of Truth, to lead us and guide us in every decision we make … big and small. He knows us better than we know ourselves, so why wouldn't we want to ask Him what we should do and then follow His advice?

It still amazes me that Jesus said it was better for Him to go so the Holy Spirit could come. How could it be any better than Jesus? But what the Lord was saying is that by the Spirit, They (the fullness of the Godhead) can all be with us at the same time … everywhere. Omnipresent and Omniscient! We will never be alone. Jesus was limited to an earthly body and could only be in one location at a time. The Holy Spirit can be everywhere, with each of us, to guide us in every area.

The truth of this still reflects the original plan of God—to offer us a hope and a future of good things—health, prosperity, and the blessed life that originated with our father in the faith, Abraham. (Jeremiah 29:11).

# CHAPTER 5

# "AS A MAN THINKS IN HIS HEART, SO IS HE."

Years ago, the Lord asked me to start a non-profit ministry. Part of our calling was to help people get off the streets and into their own places. This might have been physically possible for some, but if you don't understand what caused you to be there in the first place, your history will unfortunately repeat itself. Thus, you have to help them understand their thinking. This is when my counseling became absolutely necessary in helping them be able (choose) to make permanent changes.

However, in the many years of experience this afforded me, I realized that it wasn't just people on the streets who were repeating the same dead-end cycles. Business associates, friends, and even people that I knew in the church, who were trying to use faith and stand on the Word, were also going around some of the same emotional mountains.

So I began to pray and seek the Lord as to why this was happening. He instructed me to research the brain. As I began my study, I was amazed at what He started to show me about how we are created.

Dr. Caroline Leaf in her book, *Who Switched Off My Brain?* puts it like this, "At any one moment, your brain is creatively performing about 400 billion actions, of which you are only conscious of around 2,000. Each of these harmoniously regulated actions has both a chemical and an electrical component that are responsible for triggering emotions."[14] (Leaf 3). Dr. Leaf goes on to explain that our emotions are literally cellular signals that end up translating information into what becomes our physical reality. The way this happens is because the billions of cells in our bodies are covered with little receiver type cells which are on each cellular membrane. So when there is an incoming signal, these receivers look for the ones that they will fit into.

Now I know that's a medically, scientifically derived explanation. Let me tell you how the Lord explained it to me. He said, "Everything you have ever seen or heard, since you were in your mother's womb, has been recorded in a memory cell. When something happens to you," the signal Dr. Leaf refers to, "it looks for one of these memory cells that are the closest related to it." Thus, the "fitting" part Dr. Leaf describes.

When something happens to us the thought and our reaction are a simultaneous activity in the brain—both chemical and electrical. I asked the Lord, "How is this possible? Where does the reaction or our response come from?" The Lord went on to explain that it pulls up the closest memory cell. Whatever our reaction was for it, is the same reaction we will have for this.

This completely explained why people go around the same mountain. They are continually thinking the same thing. It also explained why when someone would come to me for counseling as an adult, the root issue (or memory cell it fit with) would be something that had happened to them when they were younger. Even though what brought them to me was a current situation, we couldn't really even deal with that until the older memory cell was evaluated and healed.

Dr. Leaf also states in *WHO SWITCHED OFF MY BRAIN?*, "As soon as you are exposed to something, especially a stressful situation, what you do next has enormous implications for your emotional and physical health and wellness. As the thought enters your brain, it passes through two highly responsive brain structures, the thalamus and the amygdala … The thalamus makes sense of the incoming information and activates the memory networks of the mind to start the 'metacognitive appraisal' of the information. This metacognitive thinking goes on beyond conscious and subconscious thinking ... This assessing of incoming information is based on your existing networks."[15] (Leaf 50). Again, these "existing networks" are the memory cells we've created since our inception.

    The interesting thing about how God revealed this to me came long before I ever heard about or read Dr. Leaf's book. Naturally, He could tell me how we think and react—the functioning of the brain—because He was the creator of it from the very beginning. If anyone understands us, it's Him. That's why the Word says, "He knows us far better than we know ourselves" (Romans 8:27). Not only from a creation standpoint, but what we have come to believe along the way through the enemy's lies or our own destructive self-talk.

## DISCOVERING UNPRODUCTIVE PATTERNS

So now that we know how the brain works and our past memory cells are still leading our responses in our current day-to-day life situations, it becomes pretty important for us to deal with those issues that caused us pain and grief from our pasts. It's not just going back to relive these unpleasant events again that brings freedom. What delivers us is now we are allowing the Holy Spirit to reveal to us what we need to do in order to receive His healing—to become free in these areas. Freedom in these areas would actually mean replacing these cells with new, productive cells, so in the future, there is something healthy for your cognitive process to draw from.

    I counseled a woman who had been divorced for several years. At the time she came to see me, she had just broken up with her boyfriend of two years. She loved this man and thought they would marry within the next year. You can imagine her surprise when they broke up. But what she told me was perceptive on her part about their relationship. In the two years they had dated, she started to see some of the same unhealthy habits develop in the boyfriend that had developed in her ex-husband after they had gotten married. She thought, "There's only one common denominator here, and it's me! Am I actually bringing this out in these men? Am I the problem?"

In a way, she was, but not because of their behavior. They had their own issues to deal with. However, because she picked men with the same "qualities" or the lack of them, this did fall on her ability to choose a healthy mate. Once we went back and examined her early relationships, we were able to find the cause of her unproductive patterns and thinking.

This brings us back to "as a man thinks, so is he." The victim, the one who doesn't address the issue for inner, emotional healing at the time of the injury, leaves themselves open to pull from those unhealthy memory cells. Thus, forming or creating a totally new way of thinking and living in the victim mentality. Do they want to continue to be the victim? They would tell you instantly, "No!" But when the thinking is messed up, you will subconsciously be drawn to the same people, abuse, drugs, alcohol, and any other addictions because it's what you know.

This also explains why women, who (if) finally break free of an alcoholic, abusive husband, will later marry someone else who has exactly the same habits or lifestyle. They're repeating what's familiar, their poor thinking sabotages their ability to choose differently, producing a continuing role of maintaining a victim status.

Many, many years ago in an early James Bond movie, it opened with James trying to rescue a woman who had been taken captive and was being held prisoner. Naturally, he had to fight off guards and others to reach the room where she was tied to a bed. He untied one arm and quickly moved around the bed to untie her other arm. Surprise! She pulled the knife out of his belt and stabbed him. Immediately the scene ended with them both standing up, looking at each other.

The next scene explained what we had just witnessed. This had actually been a simulated test for James by his superiors. He was being timed and watched so his trainers could evaluate his performance.

Obviously, he failed the test. Not just because he was stabbed, but because he hadn't taken into consideration that since she had been there for a while, her thoughts and motives may have changed. The final analysis was: she no longer wanted to be rescued. She was in agreement with her attackers.

Unfortunately, the longer we stay in an unhealthy, unproductive thinking pattern, the more we believe it's easier to just stay the way we are. Most, however, do not realize how dangerous this is. In fact, they will make sure they stay the victim because their own decisions will end up sabotaging them. Dr. Caroline Leaf in her new book, *THINK, LEARN, SUCCEED*, says it like this, "What current neuroscientific research does indicate is that we can cause structural changes in our brains through the way we think, feel, and choose. Through our customized way of thinking, we can create matter with our minds."[16] (Leaf 118)

What this means in everyday language is after a period of time, we can change our entire belief system because of our thoughts. We will actually believe things that are not true and literally do not make any sense. This is what creates irrational behavior in us. We have literally deceived ourselves into believing a false reality of life.

Take the woman prisoner from the Bond movie. She was still tied up. She was still in bondage. What would make her want to injure or kill the one person who could possibly rescue her? How can one's thinking get so confused?

The most amazing part about these individuals is even though they don't like their circumstances, they aren't willing to seek help to change. YOU can't change anyone who doesn't want to take or make the necessary steps to change themselves.

# WHY JUST "GET OVER IT" DOESN'T WORK

At times, I have heard well-known ministers preach from the platform to "Just Get Over It!" However, as I have pointed out, this isn't possible—that is in the natural. All things are possible with God, so someone could receive a miracle and the weight and heaviness associated with their past could instantly be removed through the laying on of hands and prayer.

In my mid-twenties I dealt with pretty severe depression. Several years later, when I learned about replacing the memory cells and began to change those cells, my thinking changed as a result. Then, God added his "Super" to my "natural" and I received a supernatural deliverance from the depression. Thank You, God, never to return.

When that left me, I didn't notice any difference in how I looked, but people I had worked with for years began to ask me questions like, "What have you done to yourself? Did you change your hair ... hair color? Have you lost weight?" To them, my appearance had drastically changed. What I came to realize later, when I learned about demonic spirits, was that the devil of depression had left me, and as a result, my whole countenance changed.

As long as the old memory cells remain, you will have a hard time being able to think differently, which will result in you reacting in the same ways you always have. Unfortunately, this means we usually over-react to the circumstance or situation, in less than a positive way, regardless of how much time has passed since the event occurred.

Another side-effect in one's thinking, who has a victim mentality, is a spirit of entitlement. Bottom line is: IT'S ALL ABOUT ME! I believe we are seeing this more and more in today's younger generation, which is really no fault of theirs. When you have been left to "raise" yourself because of single-parent homes, or both parents employed with no one to manage them for the majority of their day, they turn to themselves for entertainment or whatever else they may need. And the situation doesn't help itself when the parents, out of guilt, buy them everything they want to keep them happy and entertained. Thus, creating the emotional response, "I deserve this. I'm entitled."

More times than not, the companion they've turned to is their phone, with all kinds of information made available to them, which has the capacity to lead them astray.

Social media is far from being social in many ways. It doesn't have the ability to teach anyone how to be relational or to socially interact with others. We've heard we are more socially connected today than ever, but now statistics prove that this is not really true. We, in fact, are more disconnected than we've ever been.

However, that loneliness and the enemy's lies still leave a huge void in their love department. Confirmation of being loved comes in the form of gifts, videos, and other electronic devices—not in spending time with them to hear and relate to what they are going through. A love deficit will injure one emotionally for years and in every area of their lives. When there is a lack of love from our fathers and mothers, it makes it difficult to believe or receive the Father's love. After all, if the very one I can see doesn't love me, or doesn't act like they love me, why would a God I can't see love me?

Even for young Christians today. When I see the lyrics that have been written and the songs that have become so popular, it's usually about them. The sentences start with "I" and tell the story about their guilt and shame, how they don't deserve it, they're undone, etc. ... the story is about them as being worthless, regardless of the fact that they are now God's child—an Ambassador for the King and His Kingdom, according to Scripture. (2 Corinthians 5:20). Eventually, these songs will say something about God's love or His delivering them. He's in there, but usually at the end.

As I had and have come to know true worship, HE was always first. It was all about Him, not about me or my desperate struggles or pleas for help.

I think about the song that calls His love … reckless. This song has a beautiful melody and some of it is scriptural. I was in a worship service earlier last year when I heard this song for the first time. Immediately I was grieved in the Spirit. When I left the service, I heard the Holy Spirit say to me, "Look up the meaning of that word." So when I got back to my office, I looked it up.

Webster's Dictionary defines the word reckless like this,

"Marked by lack of proper caution : careless of consequences; 2: IRRESPONSIBLE …" (of a person or their actions) without thinking or caring about the consequences of an action."

Synonyms are: rash, careless, thoughtless, foolhardy, negligent, etc…

Now I ask you. Does this sound like our loving, Heavenly Father? When the Word tells us He has ordered our steps; He loved us so much that He sent His only Son to redeem us back to Him; that His own Son died to pay the cost of our sin; that He has a great plan without harm for our future …? There is nothing about God that is irresponsible. From the very beginning of Creation He has had a plan for us. And that plan has nothing to do with the lack of or a thoughtless, disregard for our future.

## A SPIRIT OF ENTITLEMENT

This spirit of entitlement is demonic, and it works side-by-side with a spirit of self-pity.

The definition of entitlement is: the belief that one is inherently deserving of privileges or special treatment.

The definition of self-pity is: excessive, self-absorbed unhappiness over one's own troubles.

You can see how both of these could lead someone down the wrong path in the way they view or think about events that happen to them and around them. Without managing their thoughts, they play right into the devil's hands.

These two demonic influences can become such a driving force that it literally causes one to become so angry that violence is sure to follow. Today, many feel they are entitled because of what they've been through, and now it becomes the world's responsibility to repay them. We see this frequently in the news in a variety of ways. Even to the degree that some would think a socialist government could be the answer. How does one think the government can pay for everything? Where do they think the money would come from?

History has sadly proven and still speaks loudly in any foreign land that has agreed to this form of leadership/government control. These countries are desolate with the people living in poverty conditions. Riots and their military are positioned everywhere, killing many who try to rise up or defend themselves.

We are witnessing a form of this now because of what has just happened. Someone has been mistreated, abused, or even killed by a policeman, and now all police are at risk, being killed or attacked everywhere by many who have no justifiable reason to be using force or violence. This anger is causing riots and protests in all U.S. cities. Innocent shop owners are being beaten, robbed, even left for dead. Key national monuments of men who gave their lives to defend the very freedom that gives these individuals the right to protest are being destroyed. Racial tension is at an all-time high again throughout the U.S. And even friendships and long-term relationships with others of a different race are being questioned—tested.

Please hear me when I say that by no means do I support any unjust or prejudiced/racist treatment of another individual ... for any reason—color, nationality, wealth, status, etc.

However, the most bazaar thing about all of this is some of these protesters are demonstrating the very thing they are against—prejudice/racism! If the policeman was (is) guilty and did something wrong because of their personal prejudice or racist ideas, why are all the police lumped into the same equation? I mean, isn't this the very thing another race faces when someone of their color or nationality does something that is considered illegal, unworthy, or of bad character, etc.? Don't they feel that they are now being judged by someone else's actions? Just because they have the same skin color, live in the same neighborhood, etc.? They certainly don't like it when that happens to them, so why do they want to be a part of or participate in the same action? Really ... is this the pattern we want to see continued? Will it change anything?

If you don't want to be judged by another person's character, then choose to be secure in who God has created you to be, and walk in the love of God for everyone, which is His command to us ... Love Him first, and Love our neighbor as ourselves.

As previously mentioned, I so admired Dr. Martin Luther King, Jr. and his actions to bring peace between the races. What must he think about all of this as he views it from his mansion in Heaven?

We certainly know it's not the Father's will, when we are to love one another, as we love ourselves. Thus, we're back to the real root of the issue—being capable of loving one's own self.

Poor thinking and a lack of love for oneself will keep this kind of disunity and judgement abounding. All of which leads to serious emotional disorders and major health concerns, not only for the individuals involved, but for society at large, as well.

CHAPTER 6

# NEGATIVE EMOTIONS PRODUCE PHYSICAL ILLNESSES

For years, patients around the world have had symptoms of diseases or illnesses, but when they go to get help, many times the doctors can't find anything physically wrong with them. How can you have the symptoms of serious arthritis, joint complications, fibromyalgia, diabetes, and other illnesses, and yet, the tests come back showing nothing? Well, medical science now has come to understand the power of our thoughts and how they produce these debilitating symptoms in our bodies.

I remember several years ago seeing a young woman as she left her apartment. She locked her door and immediately got on her phone. I thought at the time, "She couldn't even wait to talk to someone later." It was then that I heard the Holy Spirit say that this is why the cell phone has become so popular, so quickly, especially with the young. People soon realized they would never have to be *alone* again. That is as long as they had an internet connection.

Recently, the movie actress, Queen Latifa and Nick Jonas, of the Jonas brothers singers, have been doing a TV commercial for the Cigna Health Network. In it they are urging people to go for their yearly physicals. This part isn't new, but what they have added to the commercial is for the patient to be very open and honest about how they are *feeling* and what they are *thinking*. So now, even the health industry wants you to express your thoughts in order for them to better diagnose your health issues.

Cigna reports, "Thanks to remarkable new technologies and the widespread use of social media, we are more "connected" than ever before. Yet as a nation, we are also lonelier. In fact, a recent study found that a staggering 47 percent of Americans often feel alone, left out and lacking meaningful connection with others. This is true for all ages, from teenagers to older adults. The number of people who perceive themselves to be alone, isolated or distant from others has reached epidemic levels both in the United States and in other parts of the world.

"While this "epidemic" of loneliness is increasingly recognized as a social issue, what's less well recognized is the role loneliness plays as a critical determinant of health. Loneliness can be deadly: this according to former Surgeon General Vivek Murthy, among others, who has stressed the significant health threat. Loneliness has been estimated to shorten a person's life by 15 years, equivalent in impact to being obese or smoking 15 cigarettes per day. A recent study revealed a surprising association between loneliness and cancer mortality risk, pointing to the role loneliness plays in cancer's course, including responsiveness to treatments."[17]

Here again, we see the power of one's thinking and how it affects their physical health. Who would have ever thought that emotional feelings of loneliness could have the same kind of effect on the physical body as 15 cigarettes?

Bill Johnson, the current Senior Pastor of Bethel Church in Redding, California, and Randy Clark, founder of Global Awakening, wrote a book called *The Essential Guide To Healing*. They write, "Many of our great doctors and psychologists have been focusing more and more on the possible connection between bodily sickness and internal issues like bitterness, anger, hatred and jealousy. We have heard for years that 85 percent of all sickness originates in the mind—not that it is imagined, just that it has its roots in an unhealthy thought life. While those internal issues are not injected into the arm or inhaled into the lungs, they poison the life of people who were created for significance. People's creative energies are redirected into the management of unhealthy thoughts and emotions, leaving them little or nothing for living in the purpose for which they were created."[18] (Johnson, Clark 175).

Medical science has confirmed that the feelings of hatred, anger, bitterness and unforgiveness all have the power to literally make a person ill. Dr. Caroline Leaf reports, **"75% to 95% of the illnesses that plague us today are a direct result of our thought life."**

What we think about affects us physically and emotionally. It's an epidemic of toxic emotions. The average person has over 30,000 thoughts a day. Through an uncontrolled thought life, we create the conditions for illness; we make ourselves sick! Research shows that fear, all on its own, triggers more than 1,400 known physical and chemical responses and activates more than 30 different hormones. There are INTELLECTUAL and MEDICAL reasons to FORGIVE!

"Toxic waste generated by toxic thoughts causes the following illnesses: diabetes, cancer, asthma, skin problems and allergies to name just a few. Consciously control your thought life and start to detox your brain!"[19]

In my second book, *COMMUNICATION FOR LIFE— COMPLETE MAKEOVER FOR THE SOUL*, I report, "Health officials say it's only 13 percent of illnesses that come from one's diet, family history or our environment. This is why it's absolutely necessary to take control of any negative emotions. If they are left buried or ignored, the toxicity they create will show up eventually in the form of headaches, panic attacks, high blood pressure, strokes, heart attacks, cancer, tumors, different types of skin and surface rashes or illness and autoimmune disorders. These are just to name a few of the serious ailments that have been associated with deeply-rooted toxic emotions."[20] (Harder 34).

# WHY I AM SICK

Think about it. Ask the Holy Spirit to show you any area in your own life that could be causing physical symptoms. Remember, the enemy came to steal, kill and destroy. (John 10:10). This is where you have to be honest about your thoughts. Do you have unforgiveness in your heart toward anyone? Are you bitter about events in your life? Do you blame others for your situation?

Unfortunately, some who may or may not even have a relationship with God, want to blame Him when something happens. The image some even have of God is the "bad guy" in Heaven, waiting for us to do something wrong, so He can beat us up with a big stick or something. God is sovereign. He is in complete control. However, God has also given us free choice, and one cannot forget about the ruler of this world—the devil—who came to steal, kill and destroy.

Years ago, while I was flying from Dallas back to Las Vegas where I was living at the time, a gentleman was sitting beside me on the plane. In the course of our conversation he asked me what I did for a living. I told him I was the founder/director of a non-profit, Christian ministry. He didn't say anything for a few seconds, then he responded with, "I used to be an elder in my church, but I don't go anymore."

Now, I didn't say anything for a few moments. Actually, I was praying in the Spirit for wisdom and direction from the Holy Spirit. Then I asked him, "If I'm not being too personal, do you mind telling me what happened that caused you to quit going to church?"

Again he waited for a few seconds, and then he said, "My son graduated from high school and was going to college on a football scholarship. He went to school a few days early to get situated. Some of the guys on the team wanted to go 4-wheeling. So he went. His 4-wheeler hit something, and it flipped over on him. My son was killed. I just didn't understand why God would take my son."

Of course I told him how sorry I was to hear about his son. Again, I needed wisdom from the Holy Spirit as to how to address this. A few minutes later I said to him, "I want to ask you another question, but I want you to know up front you don't have to answer it." He nodded his head up and down as if to say okay.

I went on to say, "I know if you were an elder in your church you know the Word of God. The Word says, we have an enemy ... a thief ... who comes to steal, kill and destroy. It also says, we have a God ... a Father ... Who came to give us life and life more abundantly. If this is true, who do you really think it was who took your son?"

Now whether or not he would have answered me I don't know, because exactly the moment I finished asking him that question and before he could even say anything, the pilot came on the intercom and made an announcement about us landing in just a few minutes, which we did. After the Captain's announcement, he didn't say anything else to me. We both exited the plane. I didn't see where he went. However, while I was waiting for my luggage, I felt someone tap me on my arm. When I turned around and looked up, it was him. With tears in his eyes, he said "Thank you!" and hugged me.

## THE "BLAME" GAME—THE "COMPARISON" GAME

The blame game and the comparison game are two of the enemy's greatest weapons. The devil goes about like a roaring lion, trying to scare us, overwhelming us with fear, attacking us in any way he can. When we let him, by believing his lies, symptoms of sickness can and will soon follow.

Dr. Scott Hannen, DC, writes in his book, *HEALING BY DESIGN*, "When a person gets sick, he usually tries to find something to make him feel better. Most people do not think of curing the sickness; instead, they usually seek relief from the symptoms. Very seldom does a person who is ill search for the cause of his problem—that seems irrelevant because he is distracted by his immediate pain and suffering."[21] (Hannen 15)

When we have been mistreated, unfairly, and the pain is real, it's hard to want to forgive someone. As explained, it's also easy to blame others, especially if we were young when the abuse happened. Naturally our parents were supposed to be the ones protecting us, not become the perpetrators themselves. However, in either or any case of mistreatment, forgiveness **does not ever** let the individual(s) off the hook for their actions.

But you, holding that hurt inside, where it's still effecting you—years later—isn't letting you off the hook, either. It's like you're drinking the poison, but expecting them to receive the injury and die. Unforgiveness still keeps you in the role of the victim. Forgiveness is for you! Once you decide to let all of those feelings and emotions go, you will be amazed at the heaviness that will go with them.

The story of Joseph, in Genesis 39-47, is a perfect example of someone who was mistreated, and not just one time, and not just by one individual. His brothers, out of jealousy, were plotting to kill him. When Joseph's father sent him out to the field where his brothers were, little did he know it would be the last time he would see him as a young man. The brothers had initially intended to kill him, but then decided to sell him to some men who were traveling by their campsite. These men took him to Egypt where another man, Potiphar, bought him to be his slave. Later, Potiphar's wife falsely accused Joseph of trying to have sex with her, when truthfully, Joseph was running from her because of her sexual advances toward him. Ordinarily, under these same conditions, the accused individual was killed, but Joseph had favor with Potiphar. So, instead of death, he was thrown into prison.

The difference in this story of Joseph's overcoming outcome is how he maintained a proper attitude—he kept his thoughts right. Instead of being and then acting like a victim, he used his faith and worked and prayed as unto the Lord. His living quarters weren't an issue. God loved him and poured out His favor upon him. Joseph was promoted many times within the prison, and the day finally came when his gift of interpreting dreams would be recognized by the Pharaoh. On that day, he received his greatest promotion. He was not only given a wife, a new and great place to live, but was honored to receive the King's signet ring of power and authority, making him Second in Command in all of Egypt. He answered only to Pharaoh.

But that's not the end of the story. Joseph's family had been experiencing famine in Israel where they lived. So the brothers were sent to Egypt to buy food and supplies. You can only imagine how awkward and emotional this was for Joseph to see those who had betrayed him. His brothers certainly weren't expecting to see him. For all they knew he could have died. But through a series of events and testing them, Joseph finally told his brothers who he was.

> "... I am Joseph, your brother, whom you sold into slavery in Egypt. But don't be upset, and don't be angry with yourselves for selling me to this place. It was God who sent me here ahead of you to preserve your lives. This famine that has ravaged the land for two years will last five more years, and there will be neither plowing nor harvesting. God has sent me ahead of you to keep you and your families alive and to preserve many survivors. So it was God who sent me here, not you! And he is the one who made me an adviser to Pharaoh—the manager of his entire palace and the governor of all Egypt" (Genesis 45:4-8, NLT).

Joseph was able to get Pharaoh's permission to have all of the Israelites come and live on the land in Egypt. They were provided for by Joseph and his position for the rest of their lives. Joseph succeeded because he didn't think like a victim. And he didn't continue to live as one, either. He never let bitterness or anger or unforgiveness become a part of who he was. He walked in love, and God honored him for it.

Another area that his story falls into is that of interpretation. This brings us back to the flour sifter. Our souls are like sifters or filters to the body. When they become clogged or dirty with all of the negative emotions, it becomes very difficult to react rationally to life's challenges, and it also becomes difficult to hear what someone is actually saying. The words now have to be sifted through the status or area of one's filter, which will produce results based on how healthy or unhealthy it is.

This is where interpretation comes in. Many times, how we interpret or hear something is not what was actually said. Or even how the person said it, based on the health status of their emotions, may keep them from presenting it like they fully intended it to be or mean in the beginning. It wasn't presented correctly or heard correctly because both individuals had clogged filters. You can see how these conversations can escalate into something far more serious.

If Joseph wanted to interpret evil for his brothers' actions, instead of allowing it to register for the good God intended for it to be, can you see how different his life story would have been?

## DEMONIC INVOLVEMENT

In chapter two, we talked about heredity and its effects on us. When sexual sins like incest, molestation or any form of sexual, verbal or physical abuse are passed down from generation to generation, you are dealing with more than just an emotional or physical dysfunction. Exodus 20:5 states,

> "You shall not bow down to them or worship them; for
> I, the LORD your God, am a jealous God, punishing the

children for the sin of the parents to the third and fourth generation of those who hate me," (NIV).

But His Word also says that He will bless those who love Him for a thousand generations in Deuteronomy 7:9,

"Know therefore that the LORD your God is God; he is the faithful God, keeping his covenant of love to a thousand generations of those who love him and keep his commandments" (NIV).

Marilyn Hickey, the renowned national and international minister and televangelist does a great teaching on generational curses. She breaks it down like this from Proverbs 26:2, "the curse causeless does not come." She goes on to say that "the curse does not come unless there is iniquity. Iniquity is a sin that is practiced over and over until it becomes a habit. And an iniquity means to bend."[22]

She continues to describe this bending process. In other words, if we are already leaning or bending toward a specific direction in one generation, when the next generation comes up under that bend or leading, there is an even greater bending. By the time the third and fourth generation come up, the bend is so strong, they will automatically have to deal with it—from a baby. This is why I think that many who battle with their sexual identity and believe they were "born" that way are directly under this kind of a bend or bending. However, the root cause of their thinking is from a generational curse.

Years ago, I became friends with a woman I worked with who was dating another woman. She explained to me that when she was growing up she played with girls her age and didn't think anything about it. It wasn't until they got into their teens and these girls started talking about boys that she saw a difference. When they talked about how cute they were, etc., she realized she didn't feel this way about the guys; she wasn't attracted to them at all. On the other hand, she did realize that the words they were using to describe the boys were the exact words she was thinking to describe the girls. So since these feelings were there from her earliest thoughts about the opposite sex, dating, and so on, she felt like she was "born" this way. This was just who she was.

Again, this is just another example of coming up under a generational bending. By the time it has filtered down to the third and fourth generations, it has become a stronghold in their thinking patterns. These individuals wouldn't and don't know how to recognize the difference.

All the while, these demonic spirits through their stronghold will make you "feel" like a victim. Thus, leading you down the path of even more destructive thinking and self-sabotaging. However, there is hope and a release for these oppressive and manipulating spirits. His name is Jesus, and He paid a price for you and your sins when He died on the cross.

> "But Christ has rescued us from the curse pronounced by the law. When he was hung on the cross, he took upon himself the curse for our wrongdoing. For it is written in the Scriptures, 'Cursed is everyone who is hung on a tree'" (Galatians 3:13, NLT).

When we choose to accept Christ into our lives, He makes it possible for us to be delivered from these past generational curses. In fact, if you choose to accept Him, you may actually be the seed God will use to break the third or fourth generational line in your family's history.

CHAPTER 7

# OVERCOMING PAST PATTERNS

Everyone has had an opportunity to go through difficult seasons in their life. Whether you brought them on yourself through poor decisions or you were taken totally off guard, they happen. So now it's time to identify the root of your thoughts so you can move on by replacing the old negative, damaged memory cells with new, healthy ones.

Now, there are different ways to replace the old memory cells. For example, there was a book written in the mid-70s by a psychologist and a psychiatrist. The message in the book was to stop irrational thinking and turn it into rational thinking. Their book was filled with stories of their clients who had experienced horrible traumas and now lived as victims, but once they began to use what these doctors taught, they were able to move on and live productive lives.

What these doctors recommended to their patients was this. The moment something happened that was traumatic or the individual didn't like, they were to immediately stop and ask themselves, "Is this the worst thing that can happen to me?" The book taught that the "worst" thing was death because it's final. You can't change death. So when you asked yourself that question, you were really asking yourself, "Am I going to die from this situation?"

Since, of course, 99% of the time the answer was no, the next thing they were supposed to do was ask themselves, "How do I want to feel about this?" This was actually not only giving them an opportunity to deal with their feelings right at the time of the incident, but it was also giving them permission to acknowledge their feelings about it as well. For example: If you were angry, you had to decide if you wanted to kick the door down, punch your fist through the wall, or just cry! If you chose to do the latter, then you had to decide if you had cried enough or did you need to cry some more. This process kept one from ignoring or pushing the incident down within themselves. It forced you to immediately manage your thoughts and emotions.

The one amazing thing about their therapy that really worked, even though nothing about it was scriptural, is it kept one from automatically responding according to an old memory cell. By immediately asking yourself a question, it stopped the process of reacting or overreacting according to past actions from old, defective memory cells. Did it heal you from further related injury or wounds? No, it didn't, but it did help to overcome an emotional outbreak at that specific time. So it turned what could have been an irrational situation into a rational one by controlling your thoughts.

For me, the thought of death being the final or worst thing that could happen wouldn't have phased me because you can't threaten a true believer with death. Our last breath here is our first breath with the King, Jesus Christ.

The other thing about secular help is it is based on theories, even as sound and scientific as medicine has become, they are still dealing with the facts, not the truth, which is only found in God's Word. Plus, many times, they want an outside mind stimulant to be involved—drugs! When you add a drug that has the power to alternate one's thinking to an already unstable, mixed-up mind, you are adding insult to injury. This kind of therapy barely addresses the symptoms, let alone the root cause. The opioid epidemic in this country has proven this for sure. How can a drug that has the ability to trick the mind into thinking you have no pain, over time, not trick the mind into thinking or believing other things as well? I don't see how it can't have some pretty strong repercussions.

Today, the big psychological focus is on a process called Emotional Intelligence (EI), which is defined as: "the capability of recognizing one's own emotions and those of others, discern between different feelings and label them appropriately, use emotional information to guide thinking and behavior, and manage and/or adjust emotions to adapt to environments or achieve one's goal(s). Although the term first appeared in 1964 in a paper written by a member of the Department of Psychology Teachers at College Columbia University, Joel Robert Davitz, and a clinical professor of psychology in psychiatry, Michael Beldoch, it gained popularity in the 1995 book, *Emotional Intelligence*, written by author and science journalist, Daniel Goleman. Since this time, EI, and Goleman's 1995 analysis, have been criticized within the scientific community, despite prolific reports of its usefulness in the popular press."[23]

Supposedly, Daniel Goleman in this book, cited the Harvard Business School research which determined that EQ counts for twice as much as IQ and technical skills combined in determining who has the potential to be successful. So why or how could this be any kind of answer for success? Because the program instructs you to "be real" with yourself about your feelings. This may be good, but it's only the start to being free.

Yes, we have to be real with ourselves, but if we have told ourselves the same thing for a long enough period of time, are we truly capable of being honest with ourselves about how we really feel? By this time, the old memory cell is still kicking in to bring about a certain end result. And depending on how long we've told ourselves the "way" we think something happened, we truly believe it is that way.

Years ago, while I was counseling someone, I asked them to tell me what had happened to them. As they were explaining the details of the event, the Holy Spirit began to tell me what had really happened. From this I knew how to phrase the next few questions I asked them. Finally, it came to a point where I could ask, "Do you think it could have happened like this?" Then I repeated what I heard the Holy Spirit say to me. They looked at me for a second and then said, "You're right. That is exactly how it happened." The interesting part that happened next was their whole countenance changed. The truth had set them free.

Even today, I can still tell myself, "It doesn't matter." And, truthfully, the incident may not be that important in and of itself, but when there are many similar events happening, continually repeating themselves over the years, telling yourself it doesn't matter, doesn't change anything. It doesn't change your thinking ... it certainly won't change your outcome.

Pastor Steven Furtick from Elevation Church based in Charlotte, North Carolina, has a DVD series he taught called, *NOT A HOSTAGE*. The teaching comes from Philippians 1:12-26. In these verses, the Apostle Paul is talking about all the things he has suffered for Christ, at the hands of others, but it was all for good. In this stage of Paul's life, he has reached a level of progress ... he's not speaking according to what he's been through, but he's figured out what has happened to him has advanced the Gospel. Situations are going to happen in our lives that we didn't choose. This teaching makes the point, "I didn't choose it, BUT I wouldn't change it!"[24]

Paul was not a hostage—a victim—even though the Word says he had more horrible things happen to him than any other. From Paul's testimony, we can see that regardless of what happens, we have a choice about how we look at it, and ultimately, how we think about it.

The Word says in Genesis 50:20,
"You intended to harm me, but God intended it all for good ..." (NLT).

The "you" here is the devil. However, this proves to us that we have nothing to fear. God is for us and will always be there to help us, if we will call upon Him and His name.

## A SURE SOLUTION—GOD'S WORD

God and His Word are more than capable of healing you. In fact, that's what the Scripture says in Psalm 107:20.

> "He sent His word and healed them, And delivered *them* from their destructions" (NKJV).

So the way to change your memory cell is to first identify your area(s) of thinking that aren't healthy. Ask yourself, "What do I hear play over and over in my mind?" Now look at that thought. Does this line up with the Word? In other words, is this what God says about you ... or is this what someone else has said about you? Is this what the devil is trying to use as a weapon against you? Remember, he's the father of lies.

More times than not, what you are hearing doesn't agree with God's Word, nor His promises for you. This is where you use Scripture as your medicine.

## REPLACING MY THOUGHTS WITH HIS THOUGHTS

When you find yourself battling with thoughts over and over again, you must stop those thoughts and replace them with the truth of God's Word. Find verses that go against what you're trying to tell yourself. For example: If you battle with not being loved or feelings of loneliness, when you hear those thoughts try to come into your mind, you immediately quote the Word—

> I am chosen of God. (1 Peter 2:9)
> God loves me. (John 3:16).
> God called me by name and knew me from my mother's womb. (Jeremiah 1:5)
> God will never leave me nor forsake me. (Deuteronomy 31:6)

God has a great plan for my life, not to harm me, but to give me a hope and a future. (Jeremiah 29:11)

Then, thank the Holy Spirit for comforting you because He is the great comforter. (John 14:26).

Joyce Meyer, the well-known TV minister and evangelist writes in her book, *CHANGE YOUR WORDS CHANGE YOUR LIFE*, about the benefits of having the Holy Spirit living is us. "God's Spirit is in us, and His Spirit is definitely positive. We must let His Spirit do a thorough work in us, changing our thoughts and attitudes toward ourselves and working from that foundation outward until we can see all things and people the way God sees them. Even when we are doing our worst, God believes the best in regard to us, and He works with us to bring the best out of us.

"We can start by thinking and saying, 'God loves me unconditionally. He has given me His Spirit, and put a new heart and attitude in me. Everything in my spirit is good and positive and full of faith, and I will not allow the things that go on around me to dictate my attitude.' Anytime we do anything that is sinful, we should immediately ask God to forgive us and to go in a new direction. We should not ignore the wrong things that we do, but we should see and celebrate what we do that is right."[25] (Meyer 136-137).

Once you begin to listen to the Holy Spirit and start to quote the Word, out loud, over your thoughts, the enemy will quit bringing them to you—he doesn't want to hear the Word. And soon, you will have replaced those negative memory cells with the truth of God's Word.

## DAILY CONFESSIONS

In the late 70s and early 80s the charismatic churches taught the importance of daily confessions, especially if there was an area you were under attack from the enemy. Today, even when I talked about having daily confessions in the classes I taught at the Bible School, the students didn't know what I was referring to. I explained to them the importance of always speaking the Word, knowing the Word, having it ready to use at any given moment for any given circumstance. The Bible declares that the Word is powerful and can be used as a defensive weapon, like a sword.

> "For the word of God is living and active and sharper than any two-edged sword, and piercing as far as the division of soul and spirit, of both joints and marrow, and able to judge the thoughts and intentions of the heart" (Hebrews 4:12).

Just from this one Scripture we can see how powerful the Word is. The Bible also tells us that when we speak it, it will not return to us empty, but will complete what it was sent to do. (Isaiah 55:11).

The quickest way to remove old, negative memory cells is to speak the Word. We can have what we ask for in prayer if we believe we receive. (Matthew 21:22).

In Mark 11:23, we get to the root of why it's important to "speak" to our situations.

> "For verily I say unto you, That whosoever shall say unto this mountain, Be thou removed, and be thou cast into the sea; and shall not doubt in his heart, but shall believe that those things which he saith shall come to pass; he shall have whatsoever he saith" (Mark 11:23, KJV).

The interesting thing about this verse is it tells us to speak three times, but to believe only once. This just confirms what it says in Proverbs

18:21—that the power of life and death are in the tongue. When we really get a firm conviction of that, it becomes hard to speak things that don't line up or agree with God's Word. Plus, we have the benefit of God's Spirit, the Holy Spirit, living in us to lead us and guide us.

> Some daily confessions could include verses like the following:
> I have the mind of Christ. (1 Corinthians 2:16).
>
> I can do all things through Christ Who strengthens me. (Philippians 4:13).
>
> The blessings of the Lord are rich and He adds no sorrow to it. (Proverbs 10:22).
>
> Surely goodness and mercy will follow me all the days of my life. (Psalm 23:6).
>
> God did not give me a spirit of fear, but of power, love and a sound mind. (2 Timothy 1:7).
>
> You are my hiding place and my shield. I hope in your word. (Psalm 119:114).

This kind of Word therapy will change your beliefs, and increase your faith to receive your healing and wholeness in every area of your life, because faith comes by hearing, and hearing by the Word of God. (Romans 10:17).

CHAPTER 8

# FINDING COMPLETE FREEDOM

There is another area the enemy usually uses to stop us from receiving complete and total deliverance or freedom. This area is fear. The devil must have known how powerful this emotion can be or it wouldn't have been the first negative emotion to show up in the world in the Garden of Eden when Adam and Eve disobeyed God and sinned. We read the details in Genesis.

> "Now the serpent was more crafty than any of the wild animals the LORD God had made. He said to the woman, 'Did God really say, 'You must not eat from any tree in the garden?' The woman said to the serpent, 'We may eat fruit from the trees in the garden, but God did say, 'You must not eat fruit from the tree that is in the middle of the garden, and you must not touch it, or you will die. You will not certainly die,' the serpent said to the woman. 'For God knows that when you eat from it your eyes will be opened, and you will be like God, knowing good and evil.' When the woman saw that the fruit of the tree was good for food and pleasing to the eye, and also desirable for gaining wisdom, she took some and ate it. She also gave some to her husband, who was with her, and he ate it. Then the eyes of both of them were opened, and they realized they were naked; so they sewed fig leaves together

and made coverings for themselves. Then the man and his wife heard the sound of the Lord God as he was walking in the garden in the cool of the day, and they hid from the Lord God among the trees of the garden. But the Lord God called to the man, 'Where are you?' He answered, 'I heard you in the garden, and I was afraid because I was naked; so I hid.' And he said, 'Who told you that you were naked? Have you eaten from the tree that I commanded you not to eat from?' The man said, 'The woman you put here with me—she gave me some fruit from the tree, and I ate it.' Then the Lord God said to the woman, 'What is this you have done?' The woman said, 'The serpent deceived me, and I ate'" (Genesis 3:1-13, NIV).

Immediately after they disobeyed God, they knew something had changed—they were afraid. Fear also brought about blaming others—Adam blamed Eve and God, for God was the one who gave him Eve. Then Eve blamed the devil. Were both at fault? Yes, Eve and the devil were. But so was Adam. God had told him as well. He should have helped Eve when she believed the enemy's lie. Here is where we have to accept and deal with the consequences of our actions.

The real power in fear is it usually shuts us down. What it says to us, more times than not, never happens. But when you get bombarded with all of the "what ifs" it can be totally overwhelming. When mankind doesn't have an answer, doubts, inferiority, and exaggerations fill the mind.

I find it interesting in all the things God could have asked Adam and Eve, what He did ask them was, "Who told you that you were naked?" Right then, God was setting a precedence for us when we start to hear things repeatedly in our own minds. Many times we should stop and ask ourselves the same question, "Who's telling me this? Where are these thoughts coming from?"

Joyce Meyer, in her book, *CHANGE YOUR WORDS CHANGE YOUR LIFE,* gives her testimony about when she found out she had cancer. Immediately fear tried to consume her every thought and emotions. She even testifies that it was so overwhelming at times that she actually thought her knees would buckle under her. She then says, "The Holy Spirit whispered in my heart that it was important for me to speak faith and not fear."[26] (Meyer 141).

As she waited for her surgery and then the reports from the surgery, the devil tried to use both of those waiting times to continue to bombard her with fear. She says, "I don't have any secret to tell you that will keep the fearful thoughts from coming, but I do know that you don't have to receive them as your own, and speak them out of your mouth. Your mouth and your words belong to you, and you can always choose to speak what will please God and benefit you."[27] (Meyer 141).

Ecclesiastes 5:2, 3, makes it clear about what and how we are to speak.

"Do not be quick with your mouth,
do not be hasty in your heart
to utter anything before God.
God is in heaven
and you are on earth,
so let your words be few.
A dream comes when there are many cares,
and many words mark the speech of a fool" (NIV).

The Book of Ephesians also addresses our speech.
"Let there be no filthiness and silly talk, or coarse [obscene or vulgar] joking, *because* such things are not appropriate [for believers]; but instead speak of your thankfulness [to God]." (Ephesians 5:4, AMP).

Remember, we will either "Rehearse" or "Replace" those thoughts by what we say. Since we can have what we say, we need to make every word count toward receiving all the promises that God has given to you. And know as a result … you will see victory come in every area of your life!

## PRACTICE MAKES PERFECT

Anyone who has ever achieved any success in playing an instrument or the piano or in the area of sports will tell you it took discipline to practice. We only get better at something when we are willing to put some effort into it. When I was young I ran track. I won several of the competitions I competed in, but I ran and worked out every night after school to prepare. I also played several musical instruments. As any of my family members could testify to, it took much practice on my part before it was a joy to listen to me play.

This is how it is with the Word. The more we hear it, the more we know it, and the more we know it, the more it will automatically come out of our mouths the moment something happens. Besides, the Word confirms that it's faith that pleases God, and the way we increase or develop our faith is by hearing the Word.

One of the best ways I have found to renew my mind is to have the Word playing in the car or at home. There are CD's, MP3 players and phone Apps that have the Scriptures available for many different areas. Healing ones have been around for a long time. My first healing Scriptures were actually on a cassette tape. We will never go wrong playing and listening to God's Word. It's powerful, and it will accomplish what it's been sent out to do.

## TRUSTING GOD WHO IS FAITHFUL

The late Kenneth Hagin, nationally and internationally known 'Word of Faith' minister, always taught you can't operate in fear and faith at the same time. You will either think thoughts of fear, or you will cast down every idea or imagination and think what God says in His Word.

So when you start to realize you're afraid, you need to stop and ask yourself, "Why?" Even if the circumstances seem overwhelming and you're at a loss about what to do, the bottom line is … "Do you trust God?" If yes, then bring peace to yourself by quoting faith-filled words over your circumstance, family, etc.

If you don't, then why don't you? God says over 65 times in the Word for us to "Call unto Him" and He will deliver us … heal us … show us things we do not know.

He wants to help us!

However, whether you trust God in the beginning or later, the remedy is still the same. Speak the Word until peace comes, and you will see faith arise in your heart.

Jesus said it was better for Him to go so we could have the Holy Spirit. (John 16:7). The Spirit is here to lead us and guide us into all truth. He's our comforter—our helper. In John 14:16 Jesus is speaking,

"And I will pray the Father, and he shall give you another Comforter, that he may abide with you for ever;" (KJV).

John 16:13, says,
"When the Spirit of truth comes, he will guide you into all truth. He will not speak on his own, but will tell you what he has heard. He will tell you about the future." (NLT).

When we know we have the knowledge and power of the Spirit of God with us at all times, we can rest in Him and be assured that everything will be alright, even when it doesn't look that way. This is when we use our faith and don't submit to our feelings, which are fickle and unreliable.

> "For God so loved the world that he gave his one and only Son, that whoever believes in him shall not perish but have eternal life" (John 3:16, NIV).

Why would anyone be willing to sacrifice their only son to then let the receivers of this action live horrible, unproductive, fearful lives? Does this sound like love? We know it doesn't, and God truly does love us. He made His plan clear to us when He declared it in Jeremiah 29:11.

> "For I know the plans I have for you," declares the Lord, "plans to prosper you and not to harm you, plans to give you hope and a future." (NIV).

Trust God. You won't be disappointed. He loves you, and He will make a way for you where there not only doesn't seem to be a way, but it will be beyond your wildest dreams or imagination. Take every thought captive. Submit your thoughts and ways to Him. You are not a victim. Through Christ—He has made you victorious in every circumstance.

Just change your thinking, believe it, speak it, and then receive it!

# CONCLUSION

A victim is anyone who has been mistreated—unfair actions or words that have been spoken to belittle or destroy one's worth or value. A victim is anyone who has had to experience overwhelming, uncontrollable circumstances that have caused great destruction, death and despair. Today's world is widespread with these types of violations. Which means, we've all had opportunities to be a victim. It's unfortunate, but it even seems to be more of a "normal" part of life now than ever before. The question is: "What do we do after the incident or violation occurs?"

Answering this question is the hardest part because of how we have been trained, or not trained, by those who were responsible for raising us. If they over-reacted or shut-down, then more than likely, that is how we will also respond. However, regardless of how bad things may be, we still have the power to overcome every circumstance, "IF" we will learn to manage our thinking.

The thought process one goes through determines our every outcome. You may be thinking, "Can it really be that simple?" It is when you come to understand how we and our brains were created. When everything we have ever seen or heard from our mother's womb has been recorded in a memory cell, it's easy to understand why we would choose certain reactions based on past experiences. We want to lean on past experiences and training as our guide in other areas, so why wouldn't our brain do the same thing? It also goes back to the closest thought or reaction that is recorded in our cells. The only bad part or consequence to this is when the memory cells are negative, filled with pain, destruction, or are unproductive. As a result, we will continue to produce the same, self-sabotaging thoughts in our current situations.

This keeps us from being able to change our emotions; thus our circumstances, regardless of how many times we experience any kind of trauma or dysfunction. The worst part about this is what it does to our thinking. Now, we are thinking like victims, which gives our whole outlook on life a negative perspective. This is what is called a victim mentality.

You will recognize whether or not you think like a victim if you look back at your life.
- Are you repeating the same unfruitful relationships?
- Have you been divorced and married more than once?
- Can you not stay at a job for very long?
- Is the problem other co-workers' actions or words?
- Are you never appreciated?
- Do you "feel" unloved? By everyone?
- Are you always in debt? Living from paycheck to paycheck?
- Are you usually misunderstood?
- Do you blame others for your situations?

These are just a few of the battles that create permanent ways of thinking that victims have in common.

The other side effect is victims believe they are entitled to certain things because of their past, unfair or traumatic events. It has always amazed me how broken and beat up a victim can be emotionally, and yet, have such a boldness in expecting certain things to be done for them. Their lifestyle temperament is one that represents a living oxymoron.

So how does one "get off" the vicious, victim merry-go-round cycle? You must come to grips with your thoughts. The Word is clear, "As a man thinks in his heart, so is he." The only way to change your patterns is to change your thinking. First, you must analyze where the thoughts are coming from. Recognize the past events that have negative memory cells. Second, you have to replace those thoughts with the truth of God's Word. What happens to us in life are just facts. The only truth there is will be found in God's Word. All things will pass away, except God's Word, which will remain forever.

Then you must forgive those involved. The Word says God will forgive us when we forgive others. Release them, and receive freedom from your past and from them!

Once you learn and make a new habit—form new memory cells—by repeating God's Word over your situation, you will see how much easier it is to deal with certain life situations. Will there still be unfortunate circumstances? Probably so, but now you will not only have the knowledge of the Word to help you overcome and manage your emotions, but you will also have built within you a confidence and trust in God, your Father, Who loves you unconditionally. Who has a great plan for your life ... Who wants to bless you and help you to prosper in every area—family, finances, health, relationships, and so on.

Nothing changes us and overcomes our circumstances like the Word of God. The Word even declares that the angels harken to the voice of God.

> "Bless the LORD, you His angels,
> Who excel in strength, who do His word,
> Heeding the voice of His word."
> Psalm 103:20, NKJV

Now, it would only be natural that the angels would obey God if and when He told them to do something, but the Holy Spirit taught me years ago that when I speak the Word, the angels don't hear me. They hear Jesus, Who was the Word made flesh. So the angels go into action to bring about the fruition of the Words we are speaking.

John 1:14 explains it well.

"The Word became flesh and made his dwelling among us. We have seen his glory, the glory of the one and only Son, who came from the Father, full of grace and truth." (NIV).

Jesus, God's Son, came from Heaven to earth. Thirty-three years later, He paid a price on that cross for us to live victorious lives. Just as it's our choice to choose to let Him come into our hearts to be our Savior and Lord, it's our choice to let Him heal every area of our lives, beginning with our thought life.

Choose Him and His Word and be the overcomer He created you to be in every circumstance!

# —SPEAK THE WORD—
## —BELIEVE—
## —RECEIVE—

Throughout this book, the cure for overcoming a victim mentality or any negative way of thinking is to change your thinking. The way to do this is to replace the old thoughts with the truth, which is God's Word. If you battle with self-talk or things you've heard for years about yourself and want to be free, then you must do something. If you think you're right or you think you're wrong, either way you're correct.

However, when our thinking doesn't line up with what God says about us or who He's created us to be, then we have His authority and His power to change it. Now it's time to confess the Word, the truth, and change our thinking for good.

On the next few pages there are some Scriptures for you to quote over yourself … out loud … to change the way you think about yourself. They are divided into specific emotional areas. Use as many as needed from the different areas. Make them personal. Put your name in them.

Let them be your daily confession, as well as your weapon, when the enemy tries to lie to you about who you really are. You will see victory come quickly as you begin to speak the truth.

Remember …

"***Death*** and ***life*** are in ***the power*** of the ***tongue***,
And those who love it will eat its fruit" (Proverbs 18:21).

# I HAVE THE VICTORY ...

## I AM VICTORIOUS ...
Because "I CAN DO ALL THINGS THROUGH CHRIST WHO STRENGTHENS ME." Philippians 4:13

## I AM VICTORIOUS ...
Over the old me because "THEREFORE, IF ANYONE *IS* IN CHRIST, *HE IS* A NEW CREATION; OLD THINGS HAVE PASSED AWAY; BEHOLD, ALL THINGS HAVE BECOME NEW. 2 Corinthians 5:17

## I AM VICTORIOUS ...
Over every work of the enemy because "LISTEN CAREFULLY: I HAVE GIVEN YOU AUTHORITY [THAT YOU NOW POSSESS] TO TREAD ON SERPENTS AND SCORPIONS, AND [THE ABILITY TO EXERCISE AUTHORITY] OVER ALL THE POWER OF THE ENEMY (SATAN); AND NOTHING WILL [IN ANY WAY] HARM YOU." Luke 10:19

## I AM VICTORIOUS ...
Over every fear of death because "WHEN THE PERISHABLE HAS BEEN CLOTHED WITH THE IMPERISHABLE, AND THE MORTAL WITH IMMORTALITY, THEN THE SAYING THAT IS WRITTEN WILL COME TRUE: 'DEATH HAS BEEN SWALLOWED UP IN VICTORY.'

'WHERE, O DEATH, IS YOUR VICTORY? WHERE, O DEATH, IS YOUR STING?' THE STING OF DEATH IS SIN, AND THE POWER OF SIN IS THE LAW. BUT THANKS BE TO GOD! HE

GIVES US THE VICTORY THROUGH OUR LORD JESUS CHRIST." 1 Corinthians 15:54-57

## I AM VICTORIOUS ...
Over the devil, Death, Hell and the Grave because "SINCE THE CHILDREN HAVE FLESH AND BLOOD, HE TOO SHARED IN THEIR HUMANITY SO THAT BY HIS DEATH HE MIGHT BREAK THE POWER OF HIM WHO HOLDS THE POWER OF DEATH— THAT IS, THE DEVIL— AND FREE THOSE WHO ALL THEIR LIVES WERE HELD IN SLAVERY BY THEIR FEAR OF DEATH. Hebrews 2:14-15

## I AM VICTORIOUS ...
Because of the never ending power for miracles, signs and wonders through the Holy Spirit. "FOR THIS REASON I KNEEL BEFORE THE FATHER, FROM WHOM EVERY FAMILY IN HEAVEN AND ON EARTH DERIVES ITS NAME. I PRAY THAT OUT OF HIS GLORIOUS RICHES HE MAY STRENGTHEN YOU WITH POWER THROUGH HIS SPIRIT IN YOUR INNER BEING, SO THAT CHRIST MAY DWELL IN YOUR HEARTS THROUGH FAITH. AND I PRAY THAT YOU, BEING ROOTED AND ESTABLISHED IN LOVE, MAY HAVE POWER, TOGETHER WITH ALL THE LORD'S HOLY PEOPLE, TO GRASP HOW WIDE AND LONG AND HIGH AND DEEP IS THE LOVE OF CHRIST, AND TO KNOW THIS LOVE THAT SURPASSES KNOWLEDGE—THAT YOU MAY BE FILLED TO THE MEASURE OF ALL THE FULLNESS OF GOD. NOW TO HIM WHO IS ABLE TO DO IMMEASURABLY MORE THAN ALL WE ASK OR IMAGINE, ACCORDING TO HIS POWER THAT IS AT WORK WITHIN US ... Ephesians 3:14-20

# I AM MORE THAN A CONQUEROR (VICTORIOUS) THROUGH JESUS CHRIST, MY LORD …

Because "NO, IN ALL THESE THINGS WE ARE MORE THAN CONQUERORS THROUGH HIM WHO LOVED US." Romans 8:37

# GOD LOVES "YOU"

EXODUS 15:13 ... In your unfailing love you will lead the people you have redeemed. In your strength you will guide them to your holy dwelling. NIV

EXODUS 36:6 ... And he passed in front of Moses, proclaiming, "The Lord, the Lord, the compassionate and gracious God, slow to anger, abounding in love and faithfulness, maintaining love to thousands, and forgiving wickedness, rebellion, and sin." NIV

DEUTERONOMY 7:9 ... Know therefore that the Lord thy God, he is God, the faithful God, which keepeth covenant and mercy with them that love him and keep his commandments to a thousand generations. KJV

PSALM 17:7 ... Show the wonder of your great love, you who save by your right hand those who take refuge in you from their foes. NIV

PSALM 60:5 ... That thy beloved may be delivered; save with thy right hand, and hear me. KJV

PSALM 66:20 ... Praise be to God, who has not rejected my prayer or withheld his love from me! NIV

PSALM 89:28 ... I will maintain my love to him forever, and my covenant with him will never fail. NIV

PSALM 103:8 ... The Lord is compassionate and gracious, slow to anger, abounding in love. NIV

PSALM 117:2 ... For great is his love toward us, and the faithfulness of the Lord endures forever. NIV

PSALM 119:41 ... May your unfailing love come to me, O Lord, your salvation according to your promise. NIV

PSALM 136:1... O Give thanks to the Lord, for He is good; for His mercy and loving-kindness endure forever. AMP

ROMANS 5:8 ... But God demonstrates his own love for us in this: While we were still sinners, Christ died for us. NIV

ROMANS 8:38 ... For I am persuaded, that neither death, nor life, nor angels, nor principalities, nor powers, nor things present, nor things to come, Nor height, nor depth, nor any other creature, shall be able to separate us from the love of God, which is in Christ Jesus our Lord. KJV

JOHN 3:16 ... For God so loved the world, that he gave his only begotten Son, that whosoever believeth in him should not perish, but have everlasting life. KJV

EPHESIANS 2:4 ... But because of his great love for us, God, who is rich in mercy, made us alive with Christ even when we were dead in transgressions—it is by grace you have been saved. NIV

1 JOHN 3:1... How great is the love the Father has lavished on us, that we should be called the children of God! And that is what we are. NIV

1 JOHN 4:10 ... this is love: not that we loved God, but that he loved us and sent his Son as an atoning sacrifice for our sins. NIV

1 JOHN 4:16 … and so we know and rely on the love God has for us. God is love. Whoever lives in love lives in God, and God in him. NIV

1 JOHN 4:19 … We love because he first loved us. NIV

# GOD COMFORTS "YOU"

JEREMIAH 33:3 ... Call unto me, and I will answer thee, and show thee great and mighty things, which thou knowest not. KJV

PSALM 17:6 ... I call on you, O God, for you will answer me; give ear to me and hear my prayer. NIV

PSALM 18:30 ... As for God, his way is perfect; the word of the Lord is flawless. He is a shield for all who take refuge in him. NIV

PSALM 86:7 ... In the day of my trouble I will call to you, for you will answer me. NIV

PSALM 103:2-6 ... Praise the Lord, O my soul; and forget not all his benefits—who forgives all your sins and heals all your diseases, who redeems your life from the pit and crowns you with love and compassion, who satisfies your desires with good things so that your youth is renewed like the eagle's. The Lord works righteousness and justice for all the oppressed. NIV

ISAIAH 53:4-6 ... Surely he hath borne our griefs, and carried our sorrows: yet we did esteem him stricken, smitten by God, and afflicted. But he was wounded for our transgressions, he was bruised for our iniquities: the chastisement of our peace was upon him, and with his stripes we are healed. KJV

ZEPHANIAH 3:17 … The Lord your God is with you, he is mighty to save. He will take great delight in you, he will quiet you with his love, he will rejoice over you with singing. NIV

2 CORINTHIANS 1:3 … Praise be to the God and Father of our Lord Jesus Christ, the Father of compassion and the God of all comfort, who comforts us in all our troubles, so that we can comfort those in any trouble with the comfort we ourselves have received from God. NIV

EPHESIANS 2:8-10 … For it is by grace you have been saved, through faith—and this not from yourselves, it is a gift from God—not by works, so that no one can boast. For we are God's workmanship, created in Christ Jesus to do good works, which God prepared in advance for us to do. NIV

PHILIPPIANS 1:6 … being confident of this, that he who began a good work in you will carry it on to completion until the day of Christ Jesus. NIV

JOHN 14:16-17 … And I will ask the Father, and He will give you another comforter (Counselor, Helper, Intercessor, Advocate, Strengthener and Standby) that He may remain with you forever. The Spirit of Truth, Whom the world cannot receive (welcome, take to its heart), because it does not see Him, nor know and recognize Him. But you know and recognize Him, for He lives with you [constantly] and will be with you." AMP

# GOD GIVES "YOU" PEACE

EXODUS 14:13-14 ... The Lord will fight for you, and you shall hold your peace and remain at rest. AMP

NUMBERS 6:24-26 ... The Lord bless you, and watch, guard and keep you; The Lord make His face to shine upon and enlighten you and be gracious (kind, merciful, and giving favor) to you. The Lord lift up His [approving] countenance upon you and give you peace [tranquility of heart and life continually]. AMP

JOB 22:21 ... Submit to God and be at peace with him; in this way prosperity will come to you. NIV

PSALM 29:11 ... The Lord will give [unyielding and impenetrable] strength to His people; the Lord will bless His people with peace. AMP

PSALM 85:8 ... I will listen to what God the Lord will say; he promises peace to his people, his saints—but let them not return to folly. NIV

PSALM 119:165 ... Great peace have they who love Your law; nothing shall offend them or make them stumble. AMP

PROVERBS 16:7 ... When a man's ways are pleasing to the Lord, he makes even his enemies live at peace with him. NIV

ISAIAH 26:3 ... You will guard him and keep him in perfect and constant peace whose mind [both its inclination and its character] is stayed on You, because he commits himself to You, leans on You and hopes confidently in You. AMP

ISAIAH 26:12 … Lord, you establish peace for us; all that we have accomplished you have done for us. NIV

ISAIAH 32:17-18 … the fruit of righteousness will be peace; the effect of righteousness will be quietness and confidence forever. My people will live in peaceful dwelling places, in secure homes, in undisturbed places of rest. NIV

ISAIAH 54:10 … For though the mountains should depart and the hills be shaken or removed, yet My love and kindness shall not depart from you, nor shall My covenant of peace and completeness be removed, says the Lord, Who has compassion on you. AMP

JEREMIAH 33:6 … Nevertheless, I will bring health and healing to it; I will heal my people and will let them enjoy abundant peace and security. NIV

EZEKIEL 37:26 … I will make a covenant of peace with them; it will be an everlasting covenant. NIV

JOHN 14:27 … Peace I leave with you; my peace I give you. I do not give to you as the world gives. Do not let your hearts be troubled and do not be afraid. NIV

JOHN 16:33 … I have told you these things, so that in me you may have peace. In this world you will have trouble. But take heart! I have overcome the world. NIV

PHILIPPIANS 4:7 … And the peace of God, which passeth all understanding, shall keep your hearts and minds through Christ Jesus. KJV

JUDE 1:2 … May mercy, soul-peace and love be multiplied to you. AMP

# GOD GIVES "YOU" HOPE

JOB 11:18 ... You will be secure, because there is hope; you will look about you and take your rest in safety. NIV

JEREMIAH 29:11 ... For I know the plans I have for you, declares the Lord, plans to prosper you and not to harm you, plans to give you hope and a future. NIV

ZECHARIAH 9:12 ... Turn you to the stronghold [of security and prosperity], you prisoners of hope; even today do I declare that I will restore double your former prosperity to you. AMP

PSALM 25:3 ... No one whose hope is in you will ever be put to shame, NIV

PSALM 25:5 ... Guide me in your truth and teach me, for you are God my Savior, and my hope is in you all day long. NIV

PSALM 33:22 ... May your unfailing love rest upon us, O Lord, even as we put our hope in you. NIV

PSALM 119:114 ... Thou art my hiding place and my shield: I hope in thy word. KJV

PROVERBS 23:18 ... There is surely a future hope for you, and your hope will not be cut off. NIV

ISAIAH 40:31…but those who hope in the Lord will renew their strength. They will soar on wings like eagles; they will run and not grow weary, they will walk and not be faint. NIV

ROMANS 5:5 … Such hope never disappoints or deludes or shames us, for God's love has been poured out in our hearts through the Holy Spirit, Who has been given to us. AMP

ROMANS 5:13 … Now the God of hope fill you with all joy and peace in believing, that ye may abound in hope; through the power of the Holy Ghost. KJV

2 CORINTHIANS 1:10 … He has delivered us from such a deadly peril, and he will deliver us. On him we have set our hope that he will continue to deliver us. NIV

HEBREWS 6:18-19 … God did this so that, by two unchangeable things in which it is impossible for God to lie, we who have fled to take hold of the hope offered to us may be greatly encouraged. We have this hope as an anchor for the soul, firm and secure. NIV

HEBREWS 10:23 … Let us hold unswervingly to the hope we profess, for he who promised is faithful. NIV

2 THESSALONIANS 2:16-17 … May our Lord Jesus Christ himself and God our Father, who loved us and by his grace gave us eternal encouragement and good hope, encourage your hearts and strengthen you in every good deed and word. NIV

1 JOHN 3:3 … And every man that hath this hope in him purifieth himself, even as he is pure. KJV

# GOD FORGIVES "YOU"

PSALM 86:5 ... You are forgiving and good, O Lord, abounding in love to all who call to you. NIV

PSALM 32:1-2 ... Blessed is he whose transgressions are forgiven, whose sins are covered. Blessed is the man whose sin the Lord does not count against him and in whose spirit there is no deceit. NIV

PSALM 79:9 ... Help us, O God our Savior, for the glory of your name; deliver us and forgive our sins for your name's sake. NIV

PSALM 103:2-5 ... Praise the Lord, O my soul; and forget not all his benefits—who forgives all your sins and heals all your diseases, who redeems your life from the pit and crowns you with love and compassion, who satisfies your desires with good things so that your youth is renewed like the eagle's. NIV

ISAIAH 33:24 ... No one living in Zion will say, "I am ill"; and the sins of those who dwell there will be forgiven. NIV

ISAIAH 43:25 ... "I, even I, am he who blots out your transgressions, for my own sake, and remembers your sins no more. NIV

JEREMIAH 33:8 ... I will cleanse them from all the sin they have committed against me and will forgive all their sins of rebellion against me. NIV

ACTS 10:43 ... All the prophets testify about him that everyone who believes in him receives forgiveness of sins through his name. NIV

EPHESIANS 1:7-8 ... In him we have redemption through his blood, the forgiveness of sins, in accordance with the riches of God's grace that he lavished on us with all wisdom and understanding. NIV

COLOSSIANS 3:13 ... Bear with each other and forgive whatever grievances you may have against one another. Forgive as the Lord forgave you. NIV

JAMES 5:15 ... And the prayer offered in faith will make the sick person well; the Lord will raise him up. If he has sinned, he will be forgiven. NIV

1 JOHN 1:9 ... If we confess our sins, he is faithful and just to forgive us our sins, and to cleanse us from all unrighteousness. KJV

1 JOHN 2:1 ... My little children, I write you these things so that you may not violate God's law and sin; but if any one should sin, we have an Advocate (One Who will intercede for us) with the Father [it is] Jesus Christ [the all] righteous-upright, just, Who conforms to the Father's will in every purpose, thought and action. AMP

# GOD SAYS, "DO NOT BE AFRAID"

LAMENTATIONS 3:57 … You came near when I called you, and you said, "Do not fear." NIV

DEUTERONOMY 31:6 … Be strong and courageous. Do not be afraid or terrified because of them, for the Lord your God goes with you; he will never leave you nor forsake you. NIV

DEUTERONOMY 31:8 … It is the Lord that goes before you; He will [march] with you; He will not fail you or let you go, or forsake you [let there be no cowardice or flinching, but] fear not, neither become broken [in spirit] (depressed, dismayed, and unnerved with alarm). AMP

JOSHUA 1:9 … Have I not commanded you? Be strong and courageous. Do not be terrified, do not be discouraged, for the Lord your God will be with you wherever you go. NIV

PROVERBS 1:33 … but whoever listens to me will live in safety and be at ease, without fear of harm. NIV

PROVERBS 3:25 … Be not afraid of sudden terror and panic, nor of the stormy blast or the storm and ruin of the wicked when it comes [for you will be guiltless]. AMP

PROVERBS 29:25 … The fear of man brings a snare, but whoever leans on, trusts and puts his confidence in the Lord is safe and set on high. AMP

PSALM 23:4 … Yea, though I walk through the valley of the shadow of death, I will fear no evil: for thou art with me; thy rod and thy staff they comfort me. KJV

PSALM 18:3 … I will call upon the Lord, who is worthy to be praised: so shall I be saved from mine enemies. KJV

PSALM 27:1-3 … The Lord is my light and my salvation—whom shall I fear? The Lord is the stronghold of my life—of whom shall I be afraid? When evil men advance against me to devour my flesh, when my enemies and my foes attack me, they will stumble and fall. Though an army besiege me, my heart will not fear; though war break out against me, even then will I be confident. NIV

PSALM 34:4 … I sought (inquired of) for the Lord, and required Him [of necessity, and on the authority of His Word], and He heard me, and delivered me from all my fears. AMP

PSALM 34:17 … When the righteous cry for help, the Lord hears, and delivers them out of all their distress and troubles. AMP

PSALM 56:11 … In God have I put my trust, and confident reliance; I will not be afraid; what can man do to me? AMP

PSALM 91:5 … You shall not be afraid of the terror of the night, nor of the arrow [the evil plots and slanders of the wicked] that flies by day. AMP

PSALM 91:9-10 … If you make the Most High your dwelling—even the Lord, who is my refuge—then no harm will befall you, no disaster will come near your tent. NIV

PSALM 112:8 ... His heart is secure, he will have no fear; in the end he will look in triumph on his foes. NIV

PSALM 121:7-8 ... The Lord will keep you from all harm—he will watch over your life; the Lord will watch over your coming and going both now and forevermore. NIV

ISAIAH 41:10 ... So do not fear, for I am with you; do not be dismayed, for I am your God. I will strengthen you and help you; I will uphold you with my righteous right hand. NIV

ISAIAH 41:13 ... For I am the Lord, your God, who takes hold of your right hand and says to you, Do not fear; I will help you. NIV

ISAIAH 44:2 ... This is what the Lord says—he who made you, who formed you in the womb, and who will help you: Do not be afraid, O Jacob, my servant Jeshurun, whom I have chosen. NIV

ISAIAH 44:8 ... Fear not, nor be afraid [in the coming violent upheavals]; have I not told it to you from of old and declared it? And you are my witnesses! Is there a God besides me? There is no other Rock; I know not any. AMP

ISAIAH 54:14 ... You shall establish yourself on righteousness—right, in conformity with God's will and order; you shall be far even from the thought of oppression or destruction, for you shall not fear; and from terror, for it shall not come near you. AMP

MATTHEW 10:29-31 ... Are not two little sparrows sold for a penny? And yet not one of them will fall to the ground without your Father's leave and notice. But even the very hairs of your head are numbered. Fear not, then; you are of more value than many sparrows. AMP

HEBREWS 13:6 ... So that we may boldly say, The Lord is my helper, and I will not fear what man shall do unto me. KJV

PHILIPPIANS 1:28 ... And do not [for a moment] be frightened or intimidated in anything by your opponents and adversaries, for such [constancy and fearlessness] will be a clear sign [proof and seal] to them of [their impending] destruction; but [a sure token and evidence] of your deliverance and salvation, and that from God. AMP

2 TIMOTHY 1:7 ... For God hath not given us the spirit of fear; but of power, and love, and of a sound mind. KJV

1 JOHN 4:18 ... There is no fear in love—dread does not exist; but full-grown (complete, perfect) love turns fear out of doors and expels every trace of terror! For fear brings with it the thought of punishment, and [so] he who is afraid has not reached the full maturity of love—is not yet grown into love's complete perfection. AMP

# GOD'S WORD TO "YOU" ON GRIEF, SORROW & LONELINESS

DEUTERONOMY 31:6 ... Be strong and courageous. Do not be afraid or terrified because of them, for the Lord your God goes with you; he will never leave you nor forsake you. NIV

PSALM 34:18 ... The Lord is close to the brokenhearted and saves those who are crushed in spirit. NIV

PSALM 145:14 ... The Lord upholds all those who fall and lifts up all who are bowed down. NIV

PSALM 146:7-8 ... He upholds the cause of the oppressed and gives food to the hungry. The Lord sets prisoners free, the Lord gives sight to the blind, the Lord lifts up those who are bowed down, the Lord loves the righteous. NIV

PROVERBS 10:22 ... The blessing of the Lord, it maketh rich, and he addeth no sorrow with it. KJV

PROVERBS 18:24 ... A man that hath friends must show himself friendly; and there is a friend that sticketh closer than a brother. KJV

JAMES 4:8 ... Come near to God and he will come near to you. NIV

# GOD HEALS "YOU"

JEREMIAH 30:17 ... For I will restore health unto thee, and I will heal thee of thy wounds, saith the Lord. KJV

JEREMIAH 33:6 ... Nevertheless, I will bring health and healing to it; I will heal my people and will let them enjoy abundant peace and security. NIV

PSALM 18:32 ... It is God who arms me with strength and makes my way perfect. NIV

PSALM 41:3 ... The Lord will sustain him on his sickbed and restore him from his bed of illness. NIV

PSALM 103:2-3 ... Praise the Lord, O my soul, and forget not all his benefits—who forgives all your sins and heals all your diseases. NIV

PSALM 107:20 ... He sent his word, and healed them, and delivered them from their destructions. KJV

PSALM 138:3 ... In the day when I cried thou answeredst me, and strengthenedst me with strength in my soul. KJV

PSALM 146:8 ... The Lord gives sight to the blind, the Lord lifts up those who are bowed down, the Lord loves the righteous. NIV

PSALM 147:3 ... He heals the brokenhearted and binds up their wounds. NIV

PROVERBS 4:20-22 ... My son, pay attention to what I say; listen closely to my words. Do not let them out of your sight, keep them within your heart; for they are life to those who find them and health to a man's whole body. NIV

ISAIAH 35:3-4 ... Strengthen the weak hands, and make firm the feeble and tottering knees. Say to those who are of a fearful and hasty heart, Be strong, fear not! Behold, your God will come with a vengeance, with the recompense of God; He will come and save you. AMP

ISAIAH 40:29 ... He gives power to the faint; and to them that have no might he increaseth strength. (KJV)

ISAIAH 40:31 ... But they that wait upon the Lord shall renew their strength; they shall mount up with wings as eagles; they shall run, and not be weary; and they shall walk, and not faint. KJV

ISAIAH 53:4-6 ... Surely he took up our infirmities and carried our sorrows, yet we considered him stricken by God, smitten by him, and afflicted. But he was pierced for our transgressions, he was crushed for our iniquities; the punishment that brought us peace was upon him, and by his wounds we are healed. NIV

MARK 1:41 ... Filled with compassion, Jesus reached out his hand and touched the man. "I am willing," he said. "Be clean."

2 CORINTHIANS 3:17 ... Now the Lord is the Spirit, and where the Spirit of the Lord is, there is liberty—emancipation from bondage, freedom. AMP

JAMES 5:15-16 ... And the prayer [that is] of faith will save him that is sick, and the Lord will restore him; and if he has committed sins, he will be forgiven. Confess to one another therefore your faults—your slips, your false steps, your offenses, your sins; and pray [also] for one another, that you may be healed and restored—to a spiritual tone of mind and heart. The earnest (heartfelt, continued) prayer of a righteous man makes tremendous power available—dynamic in its working. AMP

3 JOHN 1:2 ... Beloved, I wish above all things that thou mayest prosper and be in health, even as thy soul prospers. KJV

# GOD GIVES "YOU" WISDOM

PROVERBS 2:6 ... For the Lord giveth wisdom: out of his mouth cometh knowledge and understanding. KJV

PROVERBS 3:1-2 ... My Son, do not forget my teaching, but keep my commands in your heart, for they will prolong your life many years and bring you prosperity. NIV

PROVERBS 4:5-6 ... Get wisdom, get understanding; do not forget my words or swerve from them. Do not forsake wisdom, and she will protect you; love her, and she will watch over you. NIV

PROVERBS 13:10 ... Pride only breeds quarrels, but wisdom is found in those who take advice. NIV

PROVERBS 19:8 ... He who gets wisdom loves his own soul; he who cherishes understanding prospers. NIV

PROVERBS 24:14 ... Know also that wisdom is sweet to your soul; if you find it, there is a future hope for you, and your hope will not be cut off. NIV

PSALM 32:8 ... I will instruct you and teach you in the way you should go; I will counsel you and watch over you. NIV

PSALM 111:10 ... The fear of the Lord is the beginning of wisdom; all who follow his precepts have good understanding. To him belongs eternal praise. NIV

LUKE 21:15 … For I will give you words and wisdom that none of your adversaries will be able to resist or contradict. NIV

JOHN 16:13 … But when He, the Spirit of Truth (the truth-giving Spirit) comes, He will guide you into all truth—the whole, full truth. For He will not speak His own message —on His own authority—but He will tell whatever He hears [from the Father, He will give the message that has been given to Him] and He will announce and declare to you the things that are to come—that will happen in the future. AMP

COLOSSIANS 2:3 … In Him all the treasures of [divine] wisdom, [of comprehensive insight into the ways and purposes of God], and [all the riches of spiritual] knowledge and enlightenment are stored up and lie hidden. AMP

JAMES 3:17 … But the wisdom from above is first of all pure (undefiled); then it is peace-loving, courteous (considerate, gentle). [It is willing to] yield to reason, full of compassion and good fruits; it is whole-hearted and straightforward, impartial and unfeigned—free from doubts, wavering and insincerity. AMP

# GOD IS "YOUR" FATHER

DEUTERONOMY 10:18 ... He executes justice for the fatherless and widow, and loves the stranger or temporary resident and gives him food and clothing. AMP

PSALM 22:9-10 ... Yet You are He Who took me out of the womb; You made me hope and trust when I was on my mother's breasts. I was cast upon You from my birth; from my mother's womb You are my God. AMP

PSALM 27:10 ... Although my father and my mother have forsaken me, yet the Lord will take me up [adopt me as his child]. AMP

PSALM 139:13-16 ... For you created my inmost being; you knit me together in my mother's womb. I praise you because I am fearfully and wonderfully made; your works are wonderful, I know that full well. My frame was not hidden from you when I was made in the secret place. When I was woven together in the depths of the earth, your eyes saw my unformed body. All the days ordained for me were written in your book before one of them came to be. NIV

PROVERBS 4:20-22 ... My son, pay attention to what I say; listen closely to my Words. Do not let them out of your sight, keep them within your heart; for they are life to those who find them and health to a man's whole body. NIV

JEREMIAH 1:5 ... Before I formed you in the womb I knew you, before you were born I set you apart; I appointed you as a prophet to the nations. NIV

ROMANS 8:14-17 … because those who are led by the Spirit of God are sons of God. For you did not receive a spirit that makes you a slave again to fear, but you received the Spirit of sonship. And by him we cry, "*Abba*, Father." The Spirit himself testifies with our spirit that we are God's children. Now if we are God's children, then we are heirs—heirs of God and co-heirs with Christ. NIV

2 CORINTHIANS 6:18 … And I will be a Father to you, and you shall be My sons and daughters, says the Lord Almighty. AMP

GALATIANS 4:4-5 … But when the time had fully come, God sent His Son, born of a woman, born under law, to redeem those under law, that we might receive the full rights of sons. NIV

GALATIANS 4:6-7 … Because you are sons, God sent the Spirit of His Son into our hearts, the Spirit who calls out, 'Abba, Father.' So you are no longer a slave, but a son; and since you are a son, God has made you also an heir. NIV

EPHESIANS 1:5 … Having predestined us into adoption of children by Jesus Christ to himself, according to the good pleasure of his will. KJV

HEBREWS 12:5-6 … And have you [completely] forgotten the divine word of appeal and encouragement in which you are reasoned with and addressed as sons? My son, do not think lightly or scorn to submit to the correction and discipline of the Lord, nor lose courage and give up and faint when you are reproved or corrected by Him; For the Lord corrects and disciplines every one whom He loves and He punishes, even scourges, every son whom He accepts and welcomes to His heart and cherishes. AMP

# GOD'S WORD TO "YOU" ON SHAME, DISGRACE & GUILT

JOB 14:14-16 ... If you put away the sin that is in your hand and allow no evil to dwell in your tent, then you will lift up your face without shame; you will stand firm and without fear. You will surely forget your trouble, recalling it only as waters gone by. NIV

PSALM 25:3 ... No one whose hope is in you will ever be put to shame, NIV

PSALM 25:20 ... Guard my life and rescue me, let me not be put to shame, for I take refuge in you. NIV

PSALM 34:5 ... Those who look to Him are radiant, their faces are never covered with shame. NIV

PSALM 44:7 ... but you give us victory over our enemies, you put our adversaries to shame. NIV

PSALM 34:22 ... The Lord redeems the life of His servants, and none of those who take refuge and trust in Him shall be condemned or held guilty. AMP

PSALM 71:24 ... My tongue will tell of your righteous acts all day long, for those who wanted to harm me have been put to shame and confusion. NIV

ISAIAH 50:7 … because the Sovereign Lord helps me, I will not be disgraced. Therefore have I set my face like flint, and I know I will not be put to shame. NIV

ISAIAH 54:4 … Do not be afraid, you will not suffer shame. Do not fear disgrace, you will not be humiliated. You will forget the shame of your youth and remember no more the reproach of your widowhood. NIV

EZEKIEL 39:26 … They will forget their shame and all their unfaithfulness they showed toward me when they lived in safety in their land with no one to make them afraid. NIV

ROMANS 8:1 … There is therefore now no condemnation to them which are in Christ Jesus, who walk not after the flesh, but after the Spirit. KJV

ROMANS 5:5 … Such hope never disappoints or deludes or shames us, for God's love has been poured out in our hearts through the Holy Spirit, Who has been given to us. AMP

ROMANS 9:33 … and the one who trusts in him will never be put to shame. NIV

ROMANS 10:11-13 … As the Scripture says, "Anyone who trusts in him will never be put to shame." For there is no difference between Jew and Gentile—the same Lord is Lord of all and richly blesses all who call on him, for, 'Everyone who calls on the name of the Lord will be saved. NIV

# GOD'S WORD TO "YOU" ON WORRY, DOUBT & ANXIETY

DEUTERONOMY 31:8 … The Lord himself goes before you and will be with you; he will never leave you nor forsake you. Do not be afraid, do not be discouraged. NIV

ZEPHANIAH 3:17 … The Lord your God is with you, he is mighty to save. He will take great delight in you, he will quiet you with his love, he will rejoice over you with singing. NIV

PSALM 9:9 … The Lord is a refuge for the oppressed, a stronghold in times of trouble. NIV

PSALM 23:4 … Yea, though I walk through the valley of the shadow of death, I will fear no evil: for thou art with me; thy rod and thy staff they comfort me. KJV

PSALM 55:22 … Cast your burden on the Lord (releasing the weight of it) and He will sustain you; he will never allow the (consistently) righteous to be moved—made to slip, fall or fail. AMP

PSALM 94:19 … When anxiety was great within me, your consolation brought joy to my soul. NIV

PROVERBS 1:33 … but whoever listens to me will live in safety and be at ease, without fear of harm. NIV

MATTHEW 11:29 ... Take My yoke upon you, and learn of me; for I am gentle (meek) and humble (lowly) in heart, and you will find rest—relief, ease and refreshment and recreation and blessed quiet—for your souls. AMP

MATTHEW 6:34 ... So do not worry or be anxious about tomorrow, for tomorrow will have worries and anxieties of its own. Sufficient for each day is its own trouble. AMP

MARK 13:11 ... Whenever you are arrested and brought to trial, do not worry beforehand about what to say. Just say whatever is given you at the time, for it is not you speaking, but the Holy Spirit. NIV

ROMANS 8:1 ... There is therefore now no condemnation to them which are in Christ Jesus, who walk not after the flesh, but after the Spirit. KJV

PHILIPPIANS 4:6 ... Do not fret or have any anxiety about anything, but in every circumstance and in everything by prayer and petition [definite requests] with thanksgiving continue to make your wants known to God. AMP

1 PETER 5:7 ... Casting the whole of your care—all your anxieties, all your worries, all your concerns, once and for all—on Him; for He cares for you affectionately, and cares about you watchfully. AMP

# GOD CORRECTS "YOU"
# AS HIS CHILD

PROVERBS 3:11-12 .... My son, do not despise the Lord's discipline and do not resent his rebuke, because the Lord disciplines those he loves, as a father the son he delights in. NIV

PROVERBS 12:1 ... Whoever loves discipline loves knowledge, but he who hates correction is stupid. NIV

PROVERBS 13:1 ... A wise son heeds his father's instruction, but a mocker does not listen to rebuke. NIV

PROVERBS 13:18 ... He who ignores discipline comes to poverty and shame, but whoever heeds correction is honored. NIV

PROVERBS 27:5 ... Better is open rebuke than hidden love. NIV

PROVERBS 27:6 ... Wounds from a friend can be trusted, but an enemy multiplies kisses. NIV

PROVERBS 28:23 ... He who rebukes a man will in the end gain more favor than he who has a flattering tongue. NIV

HEBREWS 12:5-6 ... And you have forgotten that word of encouragement that addresses you as sons: "My son, do not make light of the Lord's discipline, and do not lose heart when he rebukes you, because the Lord disciplines those he loves, and he punishes everyone he accepts as a son." Endure hardship as discipline; God is treating you as sons. For what son is not disciplined by his father? NIV

HEBREWS 12:11 ... No discipline seems pleasant at the time, but painful. Later on, however, it produces a harvest of righteousness and peace for those who have been trained by it. NIV

2 TIMOTHY 3:16-17 ... All scripture is given by inspiration of God, and is profitable for doctrine, for reproof, for correction, for instruction in righteousness: That the man of God may be perfect, thoroughly furnished unto all good works. KJV

REVELATION 3:19 ... Those whom I love I rebuke and discipline. So be earnest, and repent. NIV

# GOD'S WORD TO "YOU" ON ANGER, BITTERNESS & JEALOUSY

LEVITICUS 19:17-18 ... Do not hate your brother in your heart. Rebuke your neighbor frankly so you will not share in his guilt. Do not seek revenge or bear a grudge against one of your people, but love your neighbor as yourself. I am the Lord. NIV

PROVERBS 14:10 ... Each heart knows its own bitterness, and no one else can share its joy. NIV

PROVERBS 15:1 ... A gentle answer turns away wrath, but a harsh word stirs up anger. NIV

PROVERBS 16:32 ... He who is slow to anger is better than the mighty, and he who rules his own spirit than he who takes a city. AMP

PROVERBS 19:11 ... Good sense makes a man restrain his anger, and it is his glory to overlook a transgression or an offense. AMP

PROVERBS 29:11 ... A fool gives full vent to his anger, but a wise man keeps himself under control. NIV

PROVERBS 29:22 ... An angry man stirs up dissention, and a hot-tempered one commits many sins.

GALATIANS 5:25-26 ... If we live by the (Holy) Spirit, let us also walk by the Spirit.—If by the (Holy) Spirit we have our life [in God], let us go forward walking in line, our conduct controlled by the Spirit. Let us not become vainglorious and self-conceited, competitive and challenging and provoking and irritating to one another, envying and being jealous of one another. AMP

EPHESIANS 4:25-27 ... Therefore each of you must put off falsehood and speak truthfully to his neighbor, for we are all members of one body. "In your anger do not sin:" Do not let the sun go down while you are still angry, and so not give the devil a foothold. NIV

EPHESIANS 4:32 ... Get rid of all bitterness, rage and anger, brawling and slander, along with every form of malice. NIV

COLOSSIANS 3:7-9 ... You used to walk in these ways, in the life you once lived. But now you must rid yourselves of all such things as these: anger, rage, malice, slander, and filthy language from your lips. Do not lie to each other, since you have taken off your old self with its practices and have put on the new self, which is being renewed in knowledge in the image of its Creator. NIV

JAMES 1:19-21 ... Understand [this], my beloved brothers. Let every man be quick to hear, (a ready listener,) slow to speak, slow to take offence and to get angry. For a man's anger does not promote the righteousness God [wishes and requires]. So get rid of all uncleanness and the rampant outgrowth of wickedness, and in humble (gentle, modest) spirit receive and welcome the Word which implanted and rooted [in your hearts] contains the power to save your souls. AMP

# GOD'S WORD TO "YOU" ON FORGIVING OTHERS

MATTHEW 6:12-15 ... Forgive us our debts, as we also have forgiven our debtors. And lead us not into temptation, but deliver us from the evil one. For if you forgive men when they sin against you, your heavenly Father will also forgive you. But if you do not forgive men their sins, your Father will not forgive your sins. NIV

MATTHEW 18:21-22 ... Then came Peter to him and said, Lord, how oft shall my brother sin against me, and I forgive him? till seven times? Jesus saith unto him, "I say not unto thee, Until seven times: but, Until seventy times seven. KJV

LUKE 6:37 ... Do not judge, and you will not be judged. Do not condemn, and you will not be condemned. Forgive, and you will be forgiven.

EPHESIANS 4:32 ... Be kind and compassionate to one another, forgiving each other, just as in Christ God forgave you. NIV

COLOSSIANS 3:12-13 ... Therefore, as God's chosen people, holy and dearly loved, clothe yourselves with compassion, kindness, humility, gentleness and patience. Bear with each other and forgive whatever grievances you may have against one another. Forgive as the Lord forgave you. NIV

# GOD'S WORD TO "YOU" FOR BELIEVING "I CAN"

PROVERBS 16:3 … Roll your works upon the Lord—commit and trust them wholly to Him; [He will cause your thoughts to become agreeable to His will, and] so shall your plans be established and succeed. AMP

2 CORINTHIANS 2:14 … Now thanks be unto God, which always causeth us to triumph in Christ, and maketh manifest the savour of his knowledge by us in every place. KJV

2 CORINTHIANS 9:8 … And God is able to make all grace (every favor and earthly blessing) come to you in abundance, so that you may always and under all circumstances and whatever the need, be self-sufficient—possessing enough to require no aid or support and furnished in abundance for every good work and charitable donation. AMP

EPHESIANS 2:10 … For we are God's [own] handiwork (His workmanship) recreated in Christ Jesus, [born anew] that we may do those good works which God predestined (planned beforehand) for us, (taking paths which He prepared ahead of time) that we should walk in them—living the good life which He prearranged and made ready for us to live. AMP

PHILIPPIANS 4:13 … I can do all things through Christ which strengtheneth me. KJV

1 CORINTHIANS 10:13 … No temptation has seized you except what is common to man. And God is faithful; he will not let you be tempted

beyond what you can bear. But when you are tempted, he will also provide a way out so that you can stand up under it. NIV

2 CORINTHIANS 2:10-11 ... forgive any one anything...To keep satan from getting the advantage over us; for we are not ignorant of his wiles and intentions.

GALATIANS 5:16 ... But I say, walk and live habitually in the (Holy) Spirit—responsive to and controlled and guided by the Spirit, then you will certainly not gratify the cravings and desires of the flesh—of human nature without God. AMP

2 CORINTHIANS 10:5 ... Casting down arguments and every high thing that exalts itself against the knowledge of God, bringing every thought into captivity to the obedience of Christ. NKJV

PHILIPPIANS 4:8 ... Finally, brethren, whatever things are true, whatever things *are* noble, whatever things *are* just, whatever things *are* pure, whatever things *are* lovely, whatever things *are* of good report, if *there is* any virtue and if *there is* anything praiseworthy—meditate on these things. NKJV

COLOSSIANS 3:5-10 ... Put to death therefore what is earthly in you: sexual immorality, impurity, passion, evil desire, and covetousness, which is idolatry. On account of these the wrath of God is coming. In these you too once walked, when you were living in them. But now you must put them all away: anger, wrath, malice, slander, and obscene talk from your mouth. Do not lie to one another, seeing that you have put off the old self with its practices and have put on the new self, which is being renewed in knowledge after the image of its creator. ESV

GALATIANS 5:16-24 … But I say, walk by the Spirit, and you will not gratify the desires of the flesh. For the desires of the flesh are against the Spirit, and the desires of the Spirit are against the flesh, for these are opposed to each other, to keep you from doing the things you want to do. But if you are led by the Spirit, you are not under the law. Now the works of the flesh are evident: sexual immorality, impurity, sensuality, idolatry, sorcery, enmity, strife, jealousy, fits of anger, rivalries, dissensions, divisions, envy, drunkenness, orgies, and things like these. I warn you, as I warned you before, that those who do such things will not inherit the kingdom of God. But the fruit of the Spirit is love, joy, peace, patience, kindness, goodness, faithfulness, gentleness, self-control; against such things there is no law. And those who belong to Christ Jesus have crucified the flesh with its passions and desires. ESV

ROMANS 8:6-11 … For to set the mind on the flesh is death, but to set the mind on the Spirit is life and peace. For the mind that is set on the flesh is hostile to God, for it does not submit to God's law; indeed, it cannot. Those who are in the flesh cannot please God. You, however, are not in the flesh but in the Spirit, if in fact the Spirit of God dwells in you. Anyone who does not have the Spirit of Christ does not belong to him. But if Christ is in you, although the body is dead because of sin, the Spirit is life because of righteousness. If the Spirit of him who raised Jesus from the dead dwells in you, he who raised Christ Jesus from the dead will also give life to your mortal bodies through his Spirit who dwells in you. ESV

EPHESIANS 6:10-18 … Finally, be strong in the Lord and in his mighty power. Put on the full armor of God so that you can take your stand against the devil's schemes. For our struggle is not against flesh and blood, but against the rulers, against the authorities, against the powers of this dark world and against the spiritual forces of evil in the heavenly realms. Therefore put on the full armor of God, so that when the day of evil comes you may be able to stand your ground, and after you have done everything, to stand. Stand firm then, with the belt of truth buckled around your waist, with the breastplate of righteousness in place, and with your feet fitted with the readiness that comes from the gospel of peace. In addition to all this, take up the shield of faith, with which you can extinguish all the flaming arrows of the evil one. Take the helmet of salvation and the sword of the Spirit, which is the word of God. And pray in the Spirit on all occasions with all kinds of prayers and requests. With this in mind, be alert and always keep on praying for all the saints. NIV

HEBREWS 4:15-16 ... For we do not have a High Priest Who is unable to understand and sympathize and have a fellow feeling with our weaknesses and has been tempted in every respect as we are, yet without sinning. Let us then fearlessly and confidently and boldly draw near to the throne of grace—the throne of God's unmerited favor [to us sinners]; that we may receive mercy [for our failures] and find grace to help in good time for every need—appropriate help and well-timed help, coming just when we need it. AMP

## GOD'S WORD TO "YOU" ON SWEET SLEEP

LEVITICUS 26:6 … I will grant peace in the land and you will lie down and no one will make you afraid. NIV

DEUTERONOMY 31:6 … Be strong and courageous. Do not be afraid or terrified because of them, for the Lord your God goes with you; he will never leave you nor forsake you. NIV

JOB 3:13 … For now I would be lying down in peace; I would be asleep and at rest. NIV

JOB 11:18-19 … You will be secure, because there is hope; you will look about you and take your rest in safety. You will lie down, with no one to make you afraid, and many will court your favor. NIV

PSALM 4:8 … In peace I will both lie down and sleep, for you, Lord, alone make me dwell in safety and confident trust. AMP

PSALM 42:8 … By day the Lord directs his love, at night his song is with me—a prayer to the God of my life. NIV

PROVERBS 3:24 … When you lie down you shall not be afraid; yes, you shall lie down and your sleep will be sweet. AMP

PROVERBS 19:23 … The fear of the Lord leads to life: Then one rests content, untouched by trouble. NIV

# GOD'S WORD TO "YOU" ON BECOMING HIS CHILD

Romans 10:9, 10, states, "That if you confess with your mouth the Lord Jesus and believe in your heart that God has raised Him from the dead, you will be saved. For with the heart one believes unto righteousness, and with the mouth confession is made unto salvation."

It is the will of God the Father that all mankind—every man, woman, and child, every race, tribe, nation, and tongue be saved. He made the way simple, so all could do it, and He gave us only one way, so we wouldn't get confused. This one way is through His Son, Jesus Christ.

God sent His only begotten Son, Jesus, to come to Earth, be born of a virgin, suffer and die for our sins. Because of sin, man could not be the sacrifice, but because Jesus was sinless, He could pay the price. He was crucified and died, and on the third day He arose from the dead—defeating the devil and bringing the keys of death, hell, and the grave up with Him. He ascended into Heaven and is seated at the right hand of God the Father where He intercedes for us every moment of the day.

When we accept Jesus into our hearts, we no longer have to wonder or live in fear about anything ... especially death. We no longer have to be afraid if we will go to Heaven or hell when our physical bodies die. The moment we die our spirits will be with the Lord in Heaven.

If you would like to make Jesus the Lord and Savior of your life and receive all the benefits of a whole, healthy mind and body, financial prosperity, social well-being, and an abundant life both now and later, then pray the following prayer:

Heavenly Father, I come to You admitting that I am a sinner. I cannot save myself. I need a Savior. I ask You to forgive me of my sins and I declare to turn from my ways and follow Your ways. I believe Your Son Jesus died on the cross for my sins. I believe He rose again from the dead, so that I would be justified and made righteous through my faith in Him. I ask You now to come into my heart and to be my Lord and Savior. Thank you for washing away all my sins and making me brand new.

Hallelujah! You are now a child of God. Welcome to the family!

# THE BAPTISM IN THE HOLY SPIRIT

The Baptism of the Holy Spirit is subsequent to salvation. It is also a free gift from God for the asking. Sometimes this experience is referred to as "the Baptism of the Holy Spirit," "receiving the Spirit," or "being filled with the Spirit." They are all scriptural terms for the same experience. When we received salvation, we asked, and then accepted it by faith. It works the same way with the Baptism of the Holy Spirit. We must use our faith to receive Him.

When we receive, according to Scripture, speaking in tongues or another language other than our own is the first sign of being filled. The Word says He will give us utterance as we yield our tongue, but it is still our responsibility to speak it out. He does not take over. This is why we can stop or start speaking our heavenly language at will, and we can also sing in the Spirit when we desire.

The Baptism of the Holy Spirit accomplishes several important things in the believer's life. He strengthens and empowers our prayer life. It is His power in us that gives us the ability to overcome our sinful ways and live a godly life, and His wisdom directs not only our own lives, but He gives us knowledge to help others, so we can be a true witness for Jesus.

The Bible also says when we don't know what to pray, the Holy Spirit will make intercession through us. He always knows what to pray. If you would like to be empowered by God on High and receive this gift, pray the following prayer:

Dear Heavenly Father, I am asking you to fill me with Your Holy Spirit, so I can speak directly to You and be empowered to live a godly Christian life. I know this is a gift from You, and now I yield myself to Your Spirit and by faith I receive Him. Thank you, Lord for Your goodness to me. Amen.

Now don't use your mind because this is a spiritual experience. Just speak those few syllables or sounds you heard and God will fill you and increase your language. The Bible says praying in tongues is using your most holy faith because it isn't contaminated by your own thoughts or ideas. It's you and God—speaking Spirit to spirit.

# BIBLIOGRAPHY

1. https://www.merriam-webster.com/dictionary/victim

2. https://www.huffingtonpost.com/entry/sexual-assault-statistics_us_

3. http://www.nsvrc.org/sites/default/files/publications_nsvrc_factsheet_media-packet_statistics-about-sexual-violence_0.pdf. (f) Finkelhor, D., Hotaling, G., Lewis, I. A., & Smith, C. (1990). Sexual abuse in a national survey of adult men and women: Prevalence, characteristics and risk factors. Child Abuse & Neglect 14, 19-28. doi:10.1016/0145-2134(90)90077-7. (n) National Sexual Violence Resource Center. (2011). Child sexual abuse prevention: Overview. Retrieved from http://www.nsvrc.org/sites/default/files/Publications_ NSVRC_Overview_Child-sexual-abuse-prevention_0.pdf

4. https://en.wikipedia.org/wiki/Hurricane_Harvey

5. https://www.nytimes.com/2018/11/12/us/california-fires-camp-fire.html

6. https://www.nimh.nih.gov/health/statistics/suicide.shtml

7. https://americanaddictioncenters.org/rehab-guide/ addiction-statistics

8. "Factsheets: Incest." *Sexual Violence Free New York*. New York City Alliance Against Sexual Assault, n.d. Web. 10 Mar. 2016.

9. http://www.soc.ucsb.edu/sexinfo/article/incest-laws-united-states

10. Thompson, Ladi Peter. *THE DEVILS CALCULUS,* Frisco, Texas, R.H. Publishing, 2020.

11. Moses is honored among Jews today as the "lawgiver of Israel," and he delivers several sets of laws in the course of the four books. The first is the Covenant Code (Exodus 20:19–23:33), the terms of the covenant which God offers to the Israelites at biblical Mount Sinai.

12. https://en.wikipedia.org/wiki/Moses

13. https://en.wikipedia.org/wiki/Monkey_see,_monkey_do

14. Franklin, Jentzen. TBN Broadcast, 10:30 a.m., January 21, 2019.

15. Leaf, Dr. Caroline. *WHO SWITCHED OFF MY BRAIN?* Printed in the United States by Switch On Your Brain, South Africa, 2007.

16. Leaf, Dr. Caroline. *WHO SWITCHED OFF MY BRAIN?* Printed in the United States by Switch On Your Brain, South Africa, 2007.

17. Leaf, Dr. Caroline. *THINK, LEARN, SUCCEED.* Grand Rapids, Michigan: Baker Books, 2018.

18. https://www.cigna.com/newsroom/news-releases/2018/new-cigna-study-reveals-loneliness-at-epidemic-levels-in-america ... https://nytimes.com/2017/12/11/well/mind/how-loneliness-affects-our-health.html ... https://hbr.org/2018/10/how-peer-coaching-can-make-wirk-less-lonely ... https://press.aarp.org/2016-12-07-aarp-foundation-draws-attention-to-social-isolation-with-the-launch-of-connect2affect ... https://ascopubs.org/doi/abs/10.1200/jco.2017.35.15_suppl.10070 ... https://blogs.scientificamerican.com/observations/loneliness-is-harmful-to-our-nations-health/

19. Johnson, Bill. Clark, Randy. *The ESSENTIAL GUIDE to HEALING.* Bloomington, Minnesota: Chosen Books, 2011.

20. https://drleaf.com/about/toxic-thoughts/

21. Harder, Polly. *COMMUNICATION FOR LIFE—COMPLETE MAKEOVER FOR THE SOUL.* Lincoln, Nebraska: R.H. Publishing, 2008.

22. Hannen, Dr. Scott K. *HEALING BY DESIGN.* Lake Mary, Florida: Siloam Charisma Media/Charisma House Book Group, 2003, 2007, 2018.

23. https://www.youtube.com/watch?v=G6K6oyKTdvM

24. https://en.wikipedia.org/wiki/Emotional_intelligence

25. Furtick, Stephen. *NOT A HOSTAGE* DVD series. TBN Broadcast, 11:00 a.m., 2/4/19.

26. Meyer, Joyce. *CHANGE YOUR WORDS CHANGE YOUR LIFE.* New York, New York: Hachette Book Group, 2012.

27. Meyer, Joyce. *CHANGE YOUR WORDS CHANGE YOUR LIFE.* New York, New York: Hachette Book Group, 2012.

28. Meyer, Joyce. *CHANGE YOUR WORDS CHANGE YOUR LIFE.* New York, New York: Hachette Book Group, 2012.

# ABOUT THE AUTHOR

Polly Harder is a graduate of Rhema Bible Training Center with a degree in Pastoral Counseling. She has her Bachelor's Degree from Life Christian University in Theology and Biblical Studies and her Master's in Pastoral Ministry.

In 1993, Polly founded Jordan House Ministries, a non-profit whose vision is to help individuals with their transition from an unproductive place in their lives toward the plans and purposes God has for them. This includes mentoring and counselling men, women and young adults in many areas that can keep one emotionally bound.

She has 45+ years of entrepreneurial experience, owning six companies, and working in the marketplace in the areas of training, management, counseling, and publishing. She has taught writing classes and emotional health and wholeness classes at a Dallas-based Bible School and as a small group leader in her church.

Currently, Polly owns a publishing company where she writes, ghostwrites, and helps other authors publish their books and magazines. She has authored *Don't Be Afraid; Communication for Life—Complete Makeover For The Soul*; *Thinking About Publishing*; and *You Can Hear ME ... Conversations With God*.

For more information go to:
www.pollyharder.com
Or email:
polly.rhpublishing@gmail.com

www.ingramcontent.com/pod-product-compliance
Lightning Source LLC
Chambersburg PA
CBHW071126090426
42736CB00012B/2018